1457 PERTH AVENUE
LONDON, ONTARIO
N5V 2M4
(519) 455-5066

1457 PERTH AVENUE
LONDON, ONTARIO

D0998415

1457 PERTH AVENUE
LONDON, ONTARIO
N5V 2M4
(519) 455-5066

DRESSING UP
DRESSING DOWN

DRESSING
UP
DRESSING
DOWN

PEARL BINDER

With Drawings, Paintings, Lithographs and Prints by
PEARL BINDER
DAN JONES
FRED ELLIS
POLLY JONES
PABLO PICASSO

and Photographs by
SUSANNAH HANDLEY

London
ALLEN & UNWIN
Boston   Sydney

**Allen & Unwin (Publishers) Ltd,
40 Museum Street, London WC1A 1LU, UK**

Allen & Unwin (Publishers) Ltd,
Park Lane, Hemel Hempstead, Herts HP2 4TE, UK

Allen & Unwin Australia Pty Ltd,
8 Napier Street, North Sydney, NSW 2060, Australia

First published in 1986

British Library Cataloguing in Publication Data

Binder, Pearl
  Dressing up and dressing down.
1. Clothing and dress – History –
Pictorial works
I. Title
646.3′09   GT513
ISBN 0–04–391012–2

Set in 11 on 13 point Souvenir by Nene Phototypesetters Ltd
and printed in Great Britain by
Butler and Tanner Ltd, Frome and London

To Den and Dan
with my love

CONTENTS

	Author's Preface	*page*	xiii
1	Introduction – Symbols and Luck		1
2	The Bare Body		11
3	Birth, Marriage, Death		30
4	Jewellery		52
5	Status		67
6	Decline and Revival of Tribal & National Dress		81
7	Religious Dress		94
8	War Dress – Peace Dress – Protest Dress		118
9	Who Sets the Fashion?		136
	Postscript We Are What We Wear		152
	Index		157

LIST OF ILLUSTRATIONS

'Life emerging from the sea'   *page* xv
Carved walking stick from East Africa   2
Chinese divination symbol   3
Earliest Chinese character for food   4
Chinese children gambling   6
Lucky Chinese *Chi'i-Lin*   7
Chinese lucky tobacco pouch   8
Chelsea punks   11
Australian aborigine going walkabout   13
Australian aborigine, body painting   14
North American Indian dancers in
   body paint   15
Painted face of the Monkey Emperor   16
Lucky carved symbols on soles of statue
   of Buddha   18
Maori facial tattoo   19
Ibo dance mask   20
Padaung woman with elongated neck   23
Tight-waisted corset, 1900   25
Face painting and body painting   27
Facial ornament with animal bones   29
My first grandchild   30
Bezprizornik, homeless Russian boy   32
Irish peasant boys dressed as girls   34
Lucky babycarrier   35
Courting present of painted jugs   36

Sleeping mat with hibiscus love pattern   36
East London children playing a wedding
   game   37
Bridal painting on a winnowing tray   40
Ganesh with his mother   42
Jewish bridal outfit from the Yemen   44
Tahitian shell and feather mourning regalia   46
Village funeral   48
Britannia mourning Lord Beaconsfield   49
Fertility charm of Ashtaroth   52
Protective magic hand and foot jewels   54
The goddess Kali   55
Three symbolic rings   57
Iranian crown   58
Lucky necklaces   59
Crystal and pinchbeck trembling tiara   59
Jewelled lid for protecting food   60
Modern Iranian Imperial tiara   61
The author with Pearly King and Queen   63
Pearly royal children   64
Pearly Queen Rosie Springfield   65
Manchu cavalry influence on Chinese
   court dress   68
'The Mayor' of Newham   69
Portrait of Queen Elizabeth I   71
City dinner   73

The English middle class in Paris *page* 75
Gin-sodden children from London's
    East End   76
Unemployed in Hyde Park, 1930   78
'Breeding', *Punch* cartoon   79
Reception at Buckingham Palace   80
West Africa, silk screen print   82
Arctic Eskimo female dress   83
Indian chiefs in manacles   86
Mexican woman   88
John Bull and Uncle Sam   91
A child's drawing of God   94
Blackfoot medicine man   95
Siberian Shaman   96
Aztec worshippers in a fire ceremony   97
Bead fringe head-dress from Imperial China   99
Vevers, sacred symbols from Haiti   101
Stephen Gardner, Bishop of Winchester   103
Sunday morning in Suva, Fiji   104
A Hebrew High Priest   106
Java batik   108
The yellow star of condemnation   109
Mexican peasant on pilgrimage   110
Gypsies on the move in Central
    Europe   112–13
Poor Moroccan Jewish immigrants   114

A print of the Resurrection   117
Scarecrow   118
Mounted Crow chief   119
Trumpeter in Imperial French cent-garde   121
Military glory   122
Sir Philip Sidney   123
Evacuation scene, 1939   124
William Penn, aged 22   127
William Penn in old age   128
Poster from a recruitment office   131
CND old lady at Greenham Common   132
The March of Labour in East London   133
Miners' picket, 1974   133
National Front invade an East End school   134
The Flower of Compassion   135
'Heaven' dance club   136
A Venetian courtesan   137
West African hairdresser's signboard   138
French aristocratic hairdressing   140
Old clothes shop   143
Design for a Revolutionary male dress   145
'New Women'   148
Vogue for very tall women   150
Banaban girl dancer   152
Cormorants crippled with oil on
    their wings   156

AUTHOR'S PREFACE

Is there no end to the number of new theories about the meaning of 'fashion'? The answer is no, because theories of fashion themselves make fashion.

'Sexual allure' is one explanation of fashion, particularly well argued by my old teacher, the late James Laver; and indeed at certain times, in certain countries, in certain sections of society, this beguiling theory cannot be ignored. But does it go far enough? There are thousands of millions of human beings in the world, all wearing clothes of some sort. How are we going to understand why they wear what they wear?

Thorstein Veblen opts for the theory of 'conspicuous consumption'; Doris Langley-Moore favours that of 'rivalry'; Dr C. Willett Cunnington suggests 'psychology'. However, since there is no single theory of fashion which is fool-proof, I propose to widen the field of survey and endeavour to see dress in all its aspects through the eyes of those who wear it, and what I myself have observed in many countries over a life-time of looking.

Dress cannot be understood out of context. What you wear, how you wear it and why you wear it, depends on time and place; and I have learned as much from anthropologists (especially the late Professor Malinowski and the late J.H. Driberg), as I have learned from James Laver, Doris Langley-Moore and Dr Cunnington. I acknowledge my debt to them all, just as I acknowledge my debt to the second-hand bookstalls in Brighton where my addiction to browsing has always been richly rewarded.

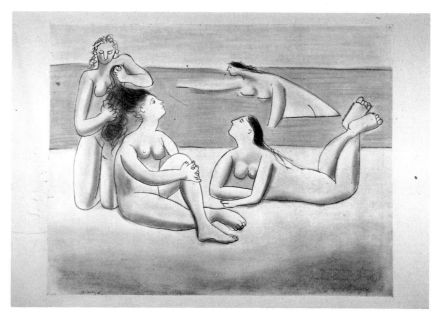

'Life emerging from the sea.' (Lithograph by Picasso – author's collection)

1 *Introduction – Symbols and Luck*

The most powerful force in the history of dress, as in all other aspects of history, is the desire to be on the winning side in the struggle for survival. King or peasant, millionaire or beggar, High Priest or atheist, slave-girl or liberated woman, they all want security, for themselves and for their families. They want to prevent any threat to that security, whether human or magic. Since what they wear is in closest personal contact to their bodies, affecting themselves directly and also seen by others as part of themselves, dress plays a vital role in their lives.

But let us begin again at the beginning.

Primitive man, struggling to survive in hot dry lands, following the trails of wild animals in his endless search for water and for edible roots and berries, sheltering in caves from heat and cold and tempest, was himself part of the animal world in a way which it is difficult for us today to understand. He was a lonely human figure in an awesome universe. His life was brief and hazardous. He begot offspring as do animals, without understanding cause and effect. He lived from day to day and was terrified of the dark.

But gradually he was beginning to raise himself above the animals because of his superior brain and because of his ability to grasp objects (potential tools like branches and flints) between his thumb and fingers. And presently he was to know fire and be able to make it and make use of it. He was becoming conscious of the immense forces of nature and their power over him. He was desperate to influence these forces to be on his side, and so eager to propitiate them.

He wanted them to act in his favour – to help him to survive – and not act against him to destroy him. He needed to communicate his wishes to the sun and the moon, to the rain, to the thunder and lightning and to the wind, to explain to all of them what he

1

wanted from them – which was warmth and food and protection.

The Australian aborigines are survivors from the Stone Age; and their approach to natural forces is respectful in precisely this way: they enter into them; they ally themselves with every aspect of plant life, animal life, and insect life; they make themselves part of the chain of nature, elaborating and sealing this affinity in dances, songs, stories and cave-paintings, chippings on rocks and paintings and collages on their own bodies. They still keep their own tribal records marked on sacred boards and they paint and chip their sacred totems on rocks on their sacred tribal sites.

Thus man's earliest surviving symbols – found not only in the great Australian deserts but on rock faces in Africa, in India, in China, in Southern America and in remote areas in Europe – however crude as they may be, are chipped with infinite care and patience, for they are *prayers*, urgent prayers, from early man to remind the elements of his human existence and to implore their mercy. They also remind him himself of his constant dependence on the elements – an anxiety he dare not neglect. He needs to ensure 'good luck'.

Should we not also remind ourselves at this point that, despite formidable technical and technological progress over thousands of years, modern man is still at the mercy of the elements? He may have walked on the moon and learned how to destroy life from huge distances, but he still cannot control the rain nor make the sun shine at his will. He cannot calm storms at sea, nor quiet earthquakes, nor quell volcanoes any better than stone-age man.

These early carved symbols of primitive man are the elements from which writing slowly developed. His earliest scripts were pictographs, Egyptian and Chinese 'picture-writing'; sometimes they are not too difficult for us to understand today, because the shapes *are* symbols. When I was travelling in China in 1960 I met the Chinese director of a new museum. She had been trained in

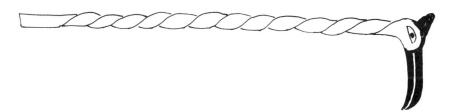

Carved walking stick
from East Africa. Head
made in England

archaeology at London University and this was her first job. She had been allotted workmen and tools and a site just outside the city and was hard at work on her dig which was already yielding treasures. As we walked around the museum she showed me her first finds, carefully displayed in new glass cases: a superb crane in red clay, eight feet high, dug up intact (the crane, intermediary between Heaven and Earth, is the Chinese symbol of immortality); and tortoise-shells for divination use. The tortoise, symbol of longevity, was equated with the vault of the sky because of its domed upper shell marked with 'constellations'. The upper shell signified Heaven = Yang (male), the flat lower shell signified Earth = Yin (female).

Chinese divination
symbol

In divining, the magician or High Priest applied heat to the tortoise-shell, interpreting, by the resulting cracks, the replies to questions. 'And this,' continued the young director, moving to the next case, 'is a good example of our very earliest Chinese writing'. With mounting excitement I stared at a piece of ancient slate covered with purposeful scratches, my eyes riveted on a repeated character – three vertical strokes above a horizontal line, below which the three vertical strokes were repeated.

3

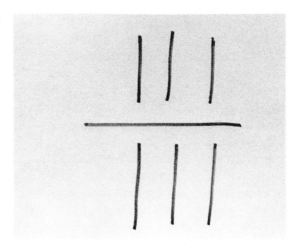

Earliest Chinese
character for food

'I think I would like to try to interpret this character, if I may,' I ventured. 'It looks to me like three stalks of growing rice reflected in water. Doesn't it signify 'food'?'

I had guessed right. That symbol, scratched by an unknown hand thousands of years ago, had spoken to me clearly. 'You couldn't possibly have understood the modern Chinese character for food,' said the Chinese director, smiling. 'It is quite different. It has evolved beyond recognition.'

That remote Chinese character for food has haunted me ever since. Repeated so insistently on a piece of slate meant surely that it was a major anxiety, as indeed food still is a major anxiety all over the world, especially in India and in Africa, subject as they are to droughts and uncontrollable floods. When such disasters strike people starve – except in the privileged Western countries, where famine today is unknown.

Food is people's constant anxiety, security their overall concern. We must expect the symbols of the illiterate common man, therefore, to focus his appeal to the Gods who control the elements upon these anxieties, imploring the Gods to prevent evil spirits from destroying his hopes of survival, from visiting him with 'bad luck'.

* Modern symbols include the genetic spiral, the CND cross and the mushroom atomic cloud.

The commonest ancient symbols are: the Circle; the Square; the Crescent; the vertical line; the horizontal line; the Cross; the triangle; and the spiral.* The oldest civilizations (all in hot dry lands) developed the richest and most intricate symbols as part of their religious rituals – elaborations of simple geometric shapes. Common man used these symbols for magical purposes – to attempt to

4

attract the powers of nature for his own needs and luck. In the words of Sir James Frazer, the author of *The Golden Bough*, the purpose of these magical attempts 'is the precise objective of true science . . . magic must be regarded as man's earliest attempt at science'.

The circle means the Sun, Eternity (a snake biting its own tail), source of all power.

The crescent means the waning moon, ship, danger (because decreasing), a Muslim religious symbol.

The square in Chinese symbolism refers to the Earth (Yin) female, or cultivation (enclosed as distinct from open nomad land).

The vertical line symbolises life, power, virility, majesty, a penis.

The horizontal line signifies to Africans Death; generally earthly concerns as opposed to spiritual concerns.

When the vertical line is crossed by the horizontal line an important new symbol is produced, which is:

The cross symbolises the act of Creation, therefore it means 'fertility' (a leap forward in human understanding of the facts of life). It also depicts the four cardinal points, an important discovery for mankind, since it stands for the 'four winds', a man at full stretch, the ancient tree of life, the Egyptian Ankh (combining male and female symbols). The cross became sacred to Christianity as the symbol of sacrifice and life eternal; but the cross is very much older than Christianity: since it symbolises the very act of creation it means all types of fertility – human, animal, and agricultural.

The triangle. The triangle pointing upward means the male, pointing downward it means the female. When superimposed one upon another they form the six-pointed star of sexual consummation, meaning fertility – a very ancient life symbol – 'Solomon's Seal', taken up by the nineteenth-century Zionists for the National Emblem of Israel. The six-pointed star also symbolises the mystic 'threes': Father, Mother, Child and Body, Soul and Spirit.

The spiral is a potent symbol connected with writhing snakes and life-giving water. It can be male, female, or self-created – lunar and solar, Yin and Yang, good and evil – life itself. It also symbolises the curling tendrils of the vine, the sacred side-curls (Paeth) of the pious Jew, also the rotation of the earth – the whirlwind (Australian desert 'willi-willi') – rainbearing clouds. In ancient Greece the spiral means the sea-shell – the rain-associated octopus – the centre of power. To the Maoris the spiral symbolised the phallus. In modern science the spiral is the genetic computer. Certain symbolic creatures have

5

Chinese children
gambling in Hong Kong.
(Lithograph by the author)

* These lucky attributes
vary – sometimes seven,
sometimes eight. In China
8 and 9 are regarded as
especially lucky numbers

survived for thousands of years and have been constantly, and still are, incorporated into dress – especially headdress – both as patterns and in the shape of garments.

The Chinese Dragon is composed of the head of a camel, horns of a stag, eyes of a demon, ears of a cow, neck of a snake, scales of a carp, paws of a tiger, belly of a frog, claws of an eagle. These nine* lucky tributes invest the Dragon with control over rainfall – a vital necessity in China. The Dragon's protruding forehead has affinities with the protruding forehead of the Buddha and is a symbol of enlightenment – by which the Dragon is enabled to soar through the air. The Dragons battle amongst the clouds in the upper air, thus producing rain.

The Chi'i-Lin is another lucky Chinese mythical creature, deriving from the giraffe first brought to China from Persia by a Muslim navigator in 1415 for the Emperor Yung-Le's private zoo. The Chi'i-Lin is regarded as a creature of good omen, appearing, like a good-conduct medal, only when China is well-governed, i.e. when her soldiers are honest and her judges upright. The Chi'i-Lin is described as being fifteen feet tall, horned, with the body of a deer, the tail of an ox, a coat of a dappled golden colour, hooved feet and a voice like a melodious bell. The Ch'i-Lin's horns punish only the guilty, always sparing the innocent. It is invisible except when Earth and Heaven are in perfect equilibrium.

6

Lucky Chinese Chi'i-Lin

The Phoenix (Feng Huang) is a mythological bird associated with Yin, the female principle, and symbolises womanly felicity. The Phoenix is six feet tall with brilliant plumage and may appear at weddings, even the poorest, to bring good luck to the bride.

Good luck – bad luck All people everywhere fear and dread 'bad luck' more than they hope and pray for 'good luck' – the poorer and more wretched their condition the more they dread bad luck, which is no stranger to them.

Today, if we are wealthy, we can clothe ourselves in the world's most sumptuous silks, costly wools and rare furs, and adorn ourselves in the world's most expensive jewels, all designed and made by the world's most distinguished designers. Yet with these

7

Chinese lucky tobacco pouch

and all the marvels of high technology available to us, we still pine for elusive good luck, waste money gambling for it, and tremble for fear of bad luck hitting us. In the 'advanced' Western world we have been brought up to take control of our environment, and to scoff at superstition: and that stern Puritan ethic, to which we are heirs, would, we might suppose, absolutely rule out any interest in 'luck'. But the reverse is the case. The very harshness of the ethic provoked and provokes its opposite – a desperate dive into the irrational, illogical, unscientific and *un*moral world of dreams, chance, and wishful thinking. The magical tales of the *Arabian Nights* were and still are related in the open air to half-starved illiterate Bedu whose harsh Muslim religion obliges them to accept their lot because it is the Will of Allah. We also know how the famous shrine in West Africa of the Thunder God Shango is besieged by successful African businessmen arriving to consult the Oracle in costly Rolls-Royce cars driven by liveried chauffeurs. But Africa, after all, is known to be still throbbing with ancient Heathen cults. Surely Britain is more enlightened? But there are many extremely expensive consultant seers living in costly apartments round about Grosvenor Square whose clients include politicians, advertising executives, bankers, company directors, lawyers. These clients have taken advice from top economists and have consulted the newest computers. And then they finally go to see their own particular fortune-teller.

Good fortune, especially when not earned, is highly esteemed. Stockbrokers who make a 'killing' are appreciated. Winners of the Pools, scoopers of lotteries, find themselves famous, applauded, respected, and fêted (riches being the main goal in our modern

Western World) *for their luck*. Everyone, on the other hand, is uneasy in the presence of 'losers'. The victims of 'bad luck' are shunned, as though they carry contagion.

For human beings at *every* stage of evolution are creatures of emotion, beset by mistrust and old, old fears. Even Freud believed in the importance of luck in human affairs; Napoleon selected his generals on their reputation of luck; and Hitler, whose ambition to dominate the world got off to such a horrifyingly successful start, used to consult necromancers.

The subject of this book is luck and how we pursue it in magic and dress, and what we wear to fend off bad luck and attract good luck. And since the subject is linked with anthropology I shall examine, amongst others, three groups of people who lived at the extremes of human endurance: first, the Polar Eskimos in the Arctic ice; second, the Banaban people, now part of Fiji, driven from their island home by foreign mining interests and losing their language, dress and pagan religion to missionaries; and third, the Australian Aborigines, surviving the fiendish heat and lack of water in the Australian desert. Human beings do not *choose* to live in such harsh surroundings. In these cases they have been driven out of better areas by force, and have had to adapt themselves to almost impossible conditions.

Daisy Bates, the anglo-Irish journalist who settled in Australia before the 1914 war to raise cattle, devoted the later part of her life and her fortune to aborigines, to their study and their care. She called herself an Anglican and respected their stone-age culture. In return they gave her their trust and confided to her their tribal secrets and sacred boards which any other woman would have been instantly killed for knowing. In her book *The Passing of the Aborigines* published in 1958 eight years after her death at the age of ninety, she wrote:

> To glean anything of value I must think with his mentality and talk in his language.

Miraculously, the aborigines of the Australian deserts have by no means passed. Today they wear whichever of white men's clothes they fancy and use his guns sometimes in hunting. But they still obey their tribal laws which, practised in secret, they have never abandoned. They are putting up a successful struggle with the Australian Government for their sacred territories.

Not long ago an Australian warden in an aborigine reserve

procured hard-board and paints for his bored charges, who had nowhere to go and nothing to do but drink. What the aborigines painted was fascinating. In quiet greys, browns, subdued yellows, near blacks, near whites, applied in small neat squares like Roman mosaics – they painted 'abstracts' which were in fact precise maps of their old desert hunting grounds. They have forgotten nothing.

The Australian aborigines have given us the boomerang* which either stunned their prey, giving the hunter time to catch up and kill it with a club, or, if it missed, came whirling back to the hand of the hunter. They have also given us the idea of the *'walk-about'* (enthusiastically adopted by British royalty); the concept of *'Dream-time'*, ancestral legends which go back further than three generations, and totems and symbols of the utmost interest in the understanding of man and the universe. They also, like other primitive people, have shown us the origins and the symbols of our dress through the manner in which they decorate their bodies.

2 *The Bare Body*

To have punctures on their skin is with them a mark of
nobility.

Herodotus
(on the Thracians)

Chelsea punks.
(Lithograph by the
author)

11

The symbols which primitive man chipped and daubed on rocks to attract the attention of the powers of nature to his needs had one serious disadvantage. They were not transportable, and primitive man was nomadic. Yet he needed to carry his messages directly to the powers of nature about with him, precisely because he was praying for help. The obvious answer was to use his own body.

So primitive man painted designs – in clay, in fruit juices, and in blood – on his body; and when he needed more permanent patterns he evolved the art of tattooing. He was eager to borrow the magic strength of birds and animals by using their natural covering and their natural weapons. There was always purpose in his actions – and always the same purpose – to survive.

The Australian aborigines, for example, painted strong designs on their dark bodies with clay – usually white clay (for white is the spirit colour) and they glued the soft white down of birds to their skin in patterns – the glue being their own blood. These designs and patterns are totemic, for each aborigine was born into a group bound together and bound into nature by their totem – an animal or bird, an insect, or plant. This totemic allegiance was absolute. It regulated and guarded their lives, shaped their laws, gave them life, gave their lives meaning and, if defied, gave them death.

I once witnessed a hunting dance at a festival in Sydney. It was danced in absolute silence by an Australian aborigine, a naked, gaunt emaciated man of middle age. His peaked forehead projecting above his alert black eyes gave him the look, to me, of a kukaburra bird. His very dark skin was strongly patterned with straight and curling designs and large spots in white clay and white birds'-down. Stalking, feinting, manoeuvring, rushing forward, stopping abruptly, then violently attacking, this aborigine, in all his inhumanly lithe movements *became* the invisible animal he was determined to kill. On this animal's death depended his food, his survival, in a hostile environment. That was the real significance of his dance.

In the Australian Central desert I once met an Aborigine family when they had left their sheep-station employment and were 'going walk-about', discarding their second-hand missionary garments gradually as they walked, just leaving them on the sand. The old man, who was their leader, limped from a long-ago hunting accident. He was carrying Aborigine weapons, spear, digging stick, boomerang, and club.

Australian aborigine
going walkabout.
(Photograph:
Hugh M. Cobbe)

There were his two wives and two little daughters – very shy and silent. All five of this Aborigine family were as thin as beanstalks. The old man, who had a few words of English, did the talking and transacting. He was courteous and sympathetic, yet somehow far away as though he and I were communicating from different levels of understanding, which I suppose we were. He was willing to sell me a flat wooden hunting club he was carrying, which I coveted, and he casually named a low price which I decided to increase for it was handsomely engraved with a spirit journey in Dreamtime.

He said he was willing to take less than the price he had asked if I paid him in coins not paper money. Exactly the same as my old London coster friends who, being out of doors in the open all day, feared paper money would blow away. Our business settled, we shared some apples and a piece of chocolate I had with me and he introduced his daughters by name – Lady and Cheechee – but not his wives.

Then they waved farewell and wandered off, shedding as they went the remainder of their white peoples' garments. Rid of this last alien distraction they looked perfectly at home in their naked dark

13

bodies on the hot red desert sand, against the harsh blue sky, on
their long journey to a distant corroboree.

The variety of richness of aborigine body decoration, indeed,
unimpeded by extremely limited materials, is a lesson to us in the
affluent countries, who possess so much and make so comparatively
little with it.

Daisy Bates explains in her book how each stage in an aborigine
boy's education was marked by different body painting, the
acquiring of different insignia *and a new name*. He was not the same

Australian aborigine,
body painting

14

person he had been before. What these boys had to learn, beginning their twenty years or more of arduous tribal initiations, was their total belonging to and commitment to their tribal totem, bound up with their nomadic life in their desert territories.

Waiting nervously to be summoned to his first initiation, an aborigine boy was painted black with charcoal (a warning to womenfolk to keep away). Until his first initiation was completed he was painted with red ochre, white clay and dark yellow ochre. His male relation mentor was also blackened with charcoal, his face was painted with vertical yellow stripes – and his forehead, nose and chin with red ochre (a clear statement of his status in the initiation ceremony).

North American Indian dancers in body paint

Many other peoples have painted their bodies and faces. They include Africans, Papuans, Ancient Britons, as well as the Plains Indians in the United States.

In traditional Chinese opera faces are now painted with their distinctive characters so that spectators will understand at a glance what behaviour to expect:

Red signifies *courage*
White signifies *treachery*
Green indicates *demons and villains*
Yellow (the imperial colour) refers to *bosses, employers*
Gilding means *Gods and immortals*
Black and white in broken pattern reveals the *neurotic character*
Black is the sign of the *disreputable person*

Painted face of the
Monkey Emperor for
Chinese traditional
opera. (Drawn by the
author)

Clowns, a survival of early values in all cultures, take their rôle so seriously that each professional clown works out his own particular painted-face, which is not allowed to copy that of any other clown. This he patents by painting it on an egg and registering it. It is remarkable how many different patterns have been invented – all instantly recognisable by their followers and fellow artists.

The Hindu equates the colour *white* (spirit life, death) with the Brahmins, their highest caste – while *red* is reserved for the Kshattriya caste, yellow for the Vaisya caste and black is for the untouchables, the outcastes. In Muslim story-telling, for instance in 'The tale of the Fisherman and the Jinni' from *The Arabian Nights* the Muslims are white, the Magians red, the Christians blue and the Jews yellow.

Since hair is magically associated with sex and potency (of the story of Samson), so is the ancient practice of dyeing the hair. For the modern development of this art, however, we should surely pay tribute to Cora Pearl, the English courtesan resident-in-France who electrified Paris during the Third Empire by inventing and using not only new colours and ways with cosmetics, but also a dazzling range of hair dye (her own hair was red and curly) from pale silver and gold through to carmine, with excursions into blue and purple. In our own time the inventive dress and textile designer Zandra Rhodes has also experimented with hair-colour. Beginning as a student, with streaks of green, now she varies her palette from delicate soap-bubble colours to vivid pink and other brilliant hues not found in nature.

Body paint or hair dye, however, can always be wiped off. So, when he was searching for more permanent marking early man invented tattooing, which, under different names, has been prac-tised throughout Polynesia and in Eastern seaports for thousands of years. It was new to Captain Cook when he and his crew first landed in Tahiti in the late eighteenth century.

A tattoo was an identification, a signature. Only important chiefs were allowed the honour of large and complicated tattoos. The process was and is very painful to endure and the resolute bearing of the pain was (and is) an essential part of the heroics of the cult.

There are ancient wall paintings showing Jewish captives with tattooing that marks their Roman ownership – like branding on cattle. Nazi Germany revived the custom when branding their Jewish and other prisoners with numbers in the concentration camps.

Tattooing today is mostly associated with young criminals, who tend to do it themselves (especially in American reformatories) with pen-nibs and permanent ink. Many punks go in for tattooing, especially coloured tattooing. It is still a very painful process but no doubt it gives them, if they feel outcast, a sense of belonging. Girls confined in jails are also likely to try tattooing. One New Mexico reform school reports that one inmate in ten is tattooed (five times more boys than girls).

Sailors and soldiers are still very likely to get tattooed during their

17

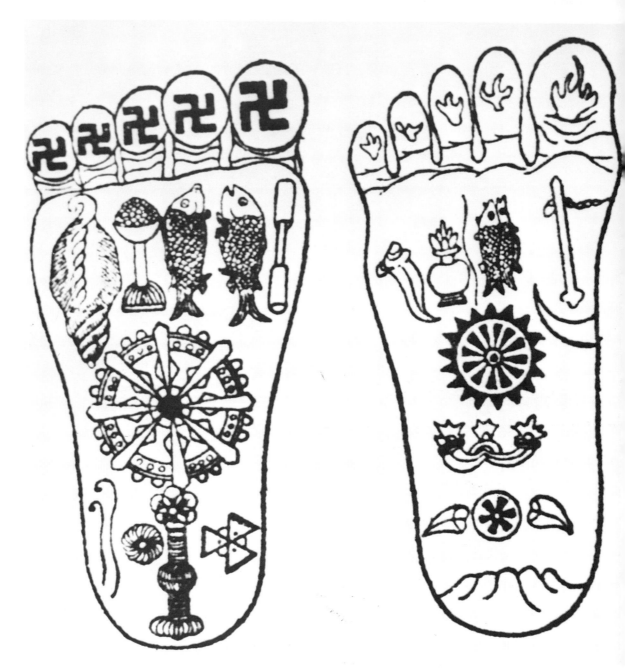

Lucky carved symbols on soles of statue of Buddha (India)

years of service. 'Mother' is more popular than the name of their sweetheart and safe too, for sweethearts change and tattooing is permanent. In the language of tattooing bluebirds may indicate the number of miles the sailor has travelled and a butterfly is the recognized emblem of the thief. Sailors I knew in the Pennyfields of

18

Maori facial tattoo,
drawn by Parkinson,
Captain Cook's
expedition

London's Chinatown in the 1930s believed that tattooing gave them immunity from smallpox, yellow fever and typhoid. A more widely spread and much earlier belief amongst European sailors was that to have a large crucifix or crucifixion picture tattooed all over his back ensured that a sailor would never be flogged, for who would dare strike a crucifix and the image of Christ with a cat-o'-nine-tails?

Coloured tattoos of great birds, dragons and beautiful flower-framed girls, require several sessions to complete and are very costly. But they are also clear evidence of manly fortitude.

A tattoo, however, can only show up on skin of light colour – the Polynesian golden coloured skin is about as deep a colour as can

Ibo dance mask
(Nigeria)

display a tattoo. For darker skins man used the art of Kelloid marking. Kelloid, which is common all over Africa – and wherever identification is required and the skin is very dark – is a process whereby the skin is cut and pricked into permanent marks and patterns, by introducing an irritant so that, on healing, the raised pattern remains – like lace.

Simple face-cutting is practised on babies of African tribes, to claim them for their tribe for always. Usually the cuts are on the cheeks, although tribes which have become Muslim are forbidden this custom. Even so it still prevails. In Africa itself Kelloid is worked on the girls' backs, breasts and upper arms in handsome patterns. The men claim that it adds to the delights of love-making to experience the feel of the lace-like texture with their hands, during the process of making love.

Primitive man not only tried to alter the appearance of his body. He also sought to alter its actual shape. This 'deformation' has been practised over the whole world in one form or another. It is done for reasons of magic – to scare away demons, to bring good luck, and, in our own culture today, it is done by both sexes in the hope of acquiring (current concepts of) beauty and attracting success and wealth. The Carrib Indians in South America pressed their babies' heads between boards (gradually and gently) to make their fore-heads slope backwards and upwards – which they believed gave them an aristocratic and, therefore, 'lucky' appearance. Semitic peoples practise the circumcision of their male babies. They claim it is for hygenic reasons, and that it affords more pleasure to both parties in love-making. But most probably it is an ancient means of tribal marking. Pious Jews believe it is a declaration of their allegiance to their God.

Female circumcision, however, can make no such claim; indeed it seems to be based on male jealousy by denying the female the pleasure of most of the clitoris in the act of love. Practitioners of female circumcision (which used to be done in East Africa with rusty razor-blades) are prepared today to allow the operation to be performed under anaesthetic in a modern surgery, but will not renounce it. Certainly it leaves scarred tissue which makes childbirth more painful and dangerous. Borneo tribes, however, *in order to please their women*, so an anthropologist, who had long worked there, told me, will fix rings of metal, bone or stone on their penises.

The Chinese (whose traditional loose dress seems to indicate a pleasure in natural lines and easy movement), for centuries used to bind the feet of their girl children where the girls of the family were not required to work in the fields. There are various legends about the origin of this custom – copying a club-footed Chinese princess is one. Another is that Li Yu, poet-king of Southern Tang (923-36) first introduced the practice because, being enamoured of a Palace entertainer Miau Niang, he believed she would dance even more gracefully if her feet were bound. She accepted the bondage of performing with her feet encased in gilded wooden gem-encrusted 'lotus' slippers, smaller than her feet. Lesser men fancied this new idea and so Chinese girl babies of good family had their feet bandaged (the toes turned backwards and tightly bound) every day for years – the bandages were only loosened for a short time to restore circulation, then put back again, and each day the bandages were tightened. The girls were consoled for their pain and

21

immobility by promises of acquiring such charm and grace that they would in due course make an excellent match.

'Golden Lotus' slippers are made of embroidered red silk, the sole (white quilted silk) being shaped like a hoof. The entire shoe measures just over two inches long. Of course ordinary walking was impossible for the owners of such 'lily' feet – and they could only totter in a dizzy way. But it seems to have been this which particularly appealed to Chinese men. Perhaps this no longer seems so outrageous a custom today, now that sex-shops reveal the fancy of many men for 'bondage' women.

Today the Chinese are ashamed and resentful of this ancient fashion, which lasted until Sun Yat Sen liberated Chinese women in 1911. In 1960, however, outside the Summer Palace I saw a middle-aged Chinese woman with 'lily' feet. What I was looking at, however, was not the pencil-shaped stumps on which she was tottering but the white puttees (a sign of mourning) in which her legs were swathed. My young interpreter, distressed, begged me not to photograph the lady – assuring me that by then 'no women under fifty in China had "lily" feet'.

Another Chinese attempt to breed a 'lucky type', was the Imperial preference for lucky *'moon faces'*. Concubines for the Imperial favour were chosen from amongst those whose faces were the roundest and fattest – for the moon was all-important to China, connected as it was with precious water and rain. One pavilion in the Imperial collection of paintings in the forbidden City of Peking is entirely devoted to exquisite paintings of Imperial concubines of that period – every one has a completely circular face, like a plate – like a moon.

Among the Padaung tribe in Burma, the women's necks have been artificially elongated, from childhood, by the addition, year by year, of brass rings. Thus the beauty of a slender female neck is exaggerated into something frightening, for these women dare not remove the brass rings because their necks have atrophied into extreme weakness and could not be held up without them. This was probably a magic practice originally, but once begun, it continuously exaggerated itself, as fashions will.

In the Victorian era in the West a quite different method of body distortion was practised upon its women. Small waists were highly esteemed and considered an essential in the marriage market. It was a period when the 'little woman' (well rounded, with side-curls and a tiny waist and little feet) was held up as the ideal. Mothers and nurses

22

Padaung woman with elongated neck. (Drawn by the author)

would lace their little girls mercilessly into tight corsets, trying for the ultimate 18-inch, even 16-inch waist. The breasts were forced up, the abdomen forced down – but not forced in, for the crinolines concealed the area between waist and ground. Cunningly the lines (diagonal) of the dresses made the waist look still smaller.

Insofar as a tiny waist might lead (as was intended) to a good marriage, the cult can be considered an attempt to attract 'luck'. But this is dangerous ground. For was it not also an unhealthy interest in pain – and in the infliction of pain? This was the period when Victorian fathers would beat their adolescent daughters and Victorian beaux delighted in tight boots, especially when 'courting'.

23

When David Copperfield was in love with Dora, for example, he wore very tight boots:

> within the first week of my passion I bought four sumptuous waistcoats – not for myself; – I had no pride in them – for Dora – and took to wearing straw-coloured kid gloves in the streets; and laid the foundations of all the corns I have ever had. If the boots I wore at that period could be produced and compared with the natural size of my feet, they would show what the state of my heart was, in a most affecting manner. And yet, wretched cripple that I had made myself by this act of homage to Dora, I walked miles upon miles daily in the hope of seeing her.

When he had made progress enough to be actually invited to Dora's house:

> I think I committed every possible absurdity in the way of preparation for this blessed event. I turn hot when I remember the cravat I bought. My boots might be placed in any collection of instruments of torture . . . But oh! when I *did* find the house, and *did* dismount at the garden gate, and drag those stony-hearted boots across the lawn to Dora, sitting on a garden seat under a lilac tree, what a spectacle she was, upon that beautiful morning among the butterflies, in a white chip bonnet and a dress of celestial blue!

In our own times groups of British youths have worn 'winklepickers' – shoes which crush and deform the feet. It is a fashion which returns constantly, as do the very high spiked heels which spoil female feet and make walking dangerous.

Surgery now offers more modern ways of changing the human shape to something fashionably pleasing. Men as well as women have 'face-lifts' to trick the years. Girls who are dissatisfied with their small breasts can have wax injections to enlarge them. (Is this an American influence – a 'mom' fantasy?) This operation was very popular in Hong Kong amongst Chinese 'joy-girls' looking for American clients, for the traditional Chinese regards a full female breast as unseemly, and slim Chinese women only develop large breasts when they are nursing their babies, their breasts resuming their seemly smallness when they have finished nursing their babies.*

Modern surgeons also offer to remodel both male and female noses. Snub? Roman? Grecian? Fashionable current T.V. star

* The cheongsam, incidentally, despite its high stiff pride-giving collar, is a Hong Kong dress, not a Chinese one; for it is short, daringly slit at the sides and very tight-fitting. It is a whore's dress directed at foreign male tourists in Hong Kong. Chinese female dress, on the other hand, however gorgeous, has always been loose and concealing.

24

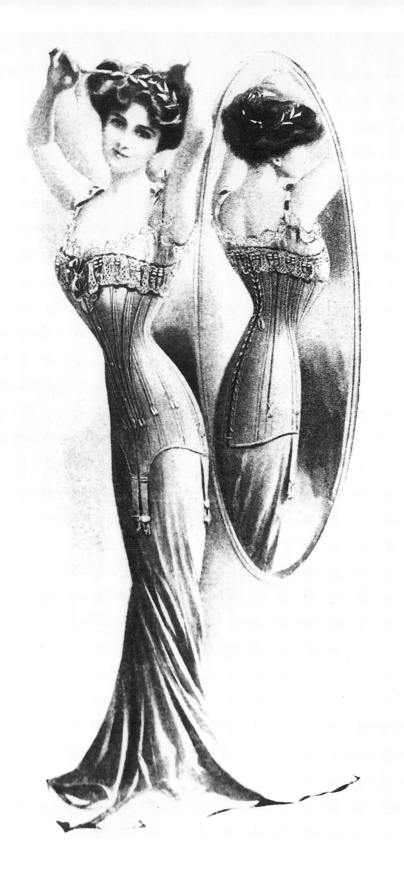

Tight-waisted
corset, 1900.
(*Brighton Recorder*)

announcer? Bottoms also. Ferocious dieting and exercising now are employed to change male and female bodies into fashionable svelte, even for those of advanced years. Short men long to be taller and have tried to achieve the illusion of height by wearing 'heighteners' inside their shoes to give them that extra inch or so. The Beatles popularised high Cuban heels for men, a fashion to which many pop groups still adhere.

Women who crave height can wear 'stilt' shoes – which also have the sexual lure of producing the tottering gait which men often seem to find irresistible. But it is not a new idea. The famous Italian Renaissance painting by Vittore Carpaccio, of two Venetian courtesans sitting on a balcony, reveals their stilt shoes.

Corsets, moreover, are not confined to women. The crack British regiments tailor their uniforms (and line and pad them) so that in effect they are corsets. Many officers in the nineteenth century, when uniforms were worn very tight and smooth, wore corsets. They were considered very manly and advertised as such in the *Tailor & Cutter*. Again, this is dangerous ground. There was immense interest during the nineteenth century in the subject of tight corsets, male and female, and pages of correspondence in the press as to the pain (delightful) and pleasure (exquisite) to be procured from wearing tight corsets. They are often associated with public school life in England and beatings by tutors, who continued the beatings begun in the nursery by nannies. Poor Swinburne never got over it.

But whatever shape man twists himself into he is at a great natural disadvantage compared with animals, birds, fishes and insects. They are not only more beautiful than he is but their natural biological weapons are much more effective. Primitive naked man, unaided, was no match for them. He lacked horns, a tail, sharp teeth, wings for flight, poison to kill or stun his adversary. He could not reproduce himself as quickly as insects, nor hope to live as long as parrots or crocodiles. But his superior brain enabled him to take their weapons from the animals and to use these weapons against them. Besides being potent weapons they also, to his mind, were imbued with magic power – the power they had possessed when part of their animal owners.

The American Plains Indians ('red' because they painted themselves with red ochre) – who were warriors and hunters of deer, bear and buffalo – were eager to obtain eagle's feathers, which they wore in their magnificent ceremonial and fighting headdresses, believing

Face painting and body painting.
American Indian warrior.
(Painting by George Catlin)

that these feathers magically bestowed on them the power of the eagles.

Not only did the warriors wear their crowns of eagles feathers but they ornamented their horses with them for the same reason. But they had, by bravery, by the number of scalps they had taken (which proclaimed, like medals, their heroic deeds) to earn the right to wear eagles' feathers and such magic-bestowing ornament. Bears' claws were a proud witness, for example, to their brave killing of the grizzly.

George Catlin's exact paintings of the Plains Indian chiefs (now in the Smithsonian collection in Washington) give us a marvellous insight into how they looked and how they lived, their ceremonies and their wars, before the white man, by superior weapons and trickery, took away their territories, destroyed the buffalo herds, and almost wiped out the tribes.

The male Plains Indian was a magnificent creature, living exactly the life most men secretly dream of, a life of short intense physical exertion hunting animals for food, fighting against his tribal enemies, adorning himself gorgeously for fabulous ceremonials, eating when he felt like eating, sleeping when he felt like sleeping, keeping his women folk under strict control to do his bidding and ease his sexual needs.

But body painting, although a primitive inheritance, is practised in many different ways in different places. In the 1950s Jane Drew, the distinguished architect, was travelling in West Africa, and was admitted to the women's quarters of the chief of a Kano district. Each of his wives had a separate small round clay and wattle dwelling where she slept, cooked, and received the Kano when he chose to visit her. The youngest and brightest wife received Jane with enthusiasm. She had not yet met any ladies from England and was eager to question her, through a lady interpreter.

After examining Jane and her appearance very closely the youngest wife demanded:

'What make-up do English ladies use?'

'Well,' replied Jane, 'we use powder, lipstick, eyebrow pencil, sometimes rouge . . .'

'Go on! Go on!' cried the youngest wife.

'Then,' continued Jane thinking hard, 'we sometimes use coloured varnish on our fingernails and toe-nails.'

'Go on! Go on!', cried the youngest wife, 'and what else?'

Jane confessed she could think of nothing else.

The Bare Body   'What about belly-painting?' demanded the young wife. 'Don't English ladies paint designs on their bellies? I hoped you would show me some new belly-painting patterns!'

Jane Drew had to admit she knew of no English ladies who painted patterns on their bellies. The youngest wife was incredulous.

'How then,' she demanded, 'do English ladies retain the interest of their husbands?'

Facial ornament with animal bones, New Guinea. (Drawn by the author)

29

3 *Birth, Marriage, Death*

Men come of age at sixty;
women at fifteen.

James Joyce

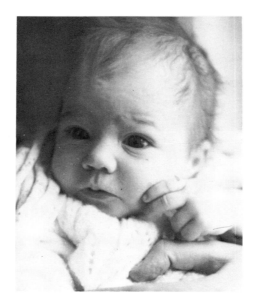

My first grandchild

Whether one is the humblest insect or an important human being, the three most important events in life are being born, becoming a parent, and dying. For all these occasions human beings need magic-protective charms and special demon-repellent dress. Survival, again, is the name of the game.

Compared to the lower orders of creation man is curiously imprudent. Insects do not propagate without providing a supply of food for their young when they hatch, whether it is a cabbage leaf or a living body. Birds do not lay their eggs until they have built a nest in which to rear their chicks, and laid claim to a food-supplying area. Even the piratical cuckoo is a good parent in providing a future for her chicks. The turtle, who never sees her offspring, yet safeguards their future by laying her eggs in the hot sand, near enough to the sustenance-rich sea into which they will scramble as soon as they hatch. Even the domesticated goldfish, swimming endlessly round in its glass bowl, is staking out its puny territorial claim to ensure food for its young.

Only man, whose sexual activity is unrestricted by seasons, does not, it seems, provide for his young. Virile young men would always rather chase a series of girls than allow themselves to be tied to one woman and take on the burden of providing for her and his children by her.

Eastern laws counter this by permitting a man to have several wives. In Africa several wives are a positive investment since, once the husband has paid for them, he sets them to work for him and can then not work himself. As the Chinese proverb expresses it, 'A teapot can pour tea into many cups but many teapots cannot pour tea into one cup.'

What matters to the community, *any* community, is that the offspring should be healthy and survive. But not all communities pursue this worthy goal in the most sensible manner. In primitive societies the woman will cease her hard outdoor toil briefly in order to give birth; then she continues to work when the baby is born. In one tribe in Papua New Guinea, the men regard childbirth with terror as an open invitation to evil spirits: a pregnant woman is therefore taboo throughout her pregnancy and, when her time comes, she has to isolate herself completely by hiding in a remote cave where she is obliged to deliver her baby herself, all alone, and attend unaided to the necessary tasks afterwards, before she is permitted to return to her tribe with her baby. There fresh taboos await her. She and her infant will be hung about with lucky demon-frustrating charms; but inevitably infant mortality is very high, being attributed to evil spirits which break through even these strong taboos.

More advanced societies are no less terrified of evil spirits and demons which may hamper the birth, exchange the infant for a changeling, or introduce evil magic through the opening by which the baby has just emerged. To counter these evil spirits (which we today would call viruses or infections) special prayers and magic rituals are performed; knots are untied, windows are opened, and anything tight is loosened – to encourage, by sympathetic magic, the baby to be born safely. Early Christians, for example, when labour was protracted, would try to ease the baby into the world by putting sweetmeats between the mother's thighs and coaxing the baby out with sweet words. In traditional Hindu and Chinese households the auspicious colour red is used for the curtains and furnishings of the delivery room. It is also very important that the female attendants at the birth should themselves be mothers of healthy sons.

Male babies are always welcome in every society. Girl babies, especially in Asia, are often unwelcome. In a Hindu household, for instance, a girl causes constant anxiety. A menstruating girl in the house brings such bad luck that she must be married before this occurs – the choice of husband dependant upon the dictates of the horoscope. If she should presently be widowed she has no

Bezprizornik, homeless Russian boy, Moscow 1930. (Drawing by Fred Ellis)

alternative but to return to her father's house, a pitiable unwanted unlucky wraith, without jewellery, in the white robes of mourning. Even worse is the case of the spinster daughter who has never married, a constant source of bad luck to the entire family.

However, the Chinese writer Wu Ching Tzu observed in his fifteenth-century novel *The Scholars:*

> Women have never been noble or base of themselves. Even a prostitute may become a concubine, while if she has a son who becomes an official she, as his mother, will be granted a noble title.

Peach-stones (peaches symbolise immortality) were a popular charm for the protection of boy babies from demons – sometimes the lucky peach-stones were made into padlocks for the child's feet 'to lock him into life'. Protective charms against evil spirits were sewn onto shoulders, breast and jackets of boy babies, and amulets made from an enormous variety of materials (gold for rich baby boys, paper or vegetable for poor peasant baby boys) were hung round their necks, often augmented with religious lucky characters printed on lucky red or yellow paper.

But even unwanted baby girls who were abandoned were not left without some ray of hope. It was customary to pin her horoscope on the baby's dress so that, should she be so fortunate as to be found and reared, it would be available when her future marriage had to be arranged.

In wealthy Chinese families a lucky malachite charm was given to the baby boy to play with, shaped like a marshall's baton. Girls were given a miniature spindle. Every effort was made to induce the Chinese bride to start a family. If, after the regulation period of gestation the bride had not given birth to a son, she would be sent 'encouraging' gifts on chosen 'lucky days' (5th to 14th of 1st month) – a paper lantern painted with a picture of Kuan Yin, the Goddess of Mercy, carrying a child, inscribed, 'May Kuan Yin present you with a son'. She might also be sent oysters which in the local dialect has the same sound as 'younger brother' – the earthenware dish holding them meaning in patois 'to come'; also rice-cakes, oranges and lucky garlic, all of which encourage children and grandchildren.

If the second year of marriage still finds the young wife without the desired son, a lantern with a stronger wish is given to her – if she is still without a son by the third year of marriage the gift lantern takes the form of an orange meaning simply 'Hurry Up!'

Every society develops its own techniques for survival. In harsh

33

Irish peasant boys
dressed as girls

polar climates Polar Eskimo mothers, in starvation time when there
was no game, would kill their beloved children rather than watch
them die agonisingly of hunger. But even in the 1940s, in cultured
Leningrad, besieged by the German army in World War II, food
became so scarce that families had to make the fearful choice of
which member should be given the chance to live.

No mother anywhere could fail to understand the deep emotion
behind this particular mother's song of the Polar Eskimos:

> It is so still in the house
> There is a calm in the house
> The snowstorm wails out there
> And the dogs are rolled up with
> Snouts under the tail
> My little boy is sleeping on the ledge
> On his back he lies, breathing
> Through his open mouth.
> Is it strange if I start
> To cry with joy?*

* *Book of the Eskimos* by
Peter Freuchen (World Pub-
lishing Company 1957)

34

She must breastfeed him for years – even into his teens if food is scarce and she is not again pregnant. But at least he would grow into a hunter, who could provide food and, just as important, sealskins or bearskins for clothes.

Babies allowed to live need help to survive in our dangerous world, where demons are always ready to pounce, especially on the more vulnerable boy babies. The Polar Eskimos used to hang the raven's claw round the neck of their baby sons – so that the raven's remarkable ability to survive in a harsh environment would pass into the child. The red cotton slings for carrying Chinese babies on their mothers' backs are always embroidered with lucky 'long life' characters.

Calling boy babies by girls' names in order to deceive the hungry demons only works for a time. All over Europe boys used not to be counted as boys until they reached the age of seven when they were officially 'breeched' and became part of the male world. Until then they wore girls' dress and their hair was coiffed like girls' hair. This prudent custom covered all boys from all classes. Examine family portraits from the sixteenth to the nineteenth centuries and it is only possible to identify the boys by the toys they carry (whips or toy horses, for example), for their hair and dress are exactly like their sisters'; and nineteenth-century village photographs reveal sturdy farmers' lads six years old or so dressed in petticoats and frocks. This precaution lasted even until 1914.

Marriage

Marriage and the begetting of children is encrusted with customs revealing hopes and fears – usually more fears than hopes – for so much can go wrong and human survival, as always, is at stake.

In Polynesian islands, before the missionaries arrived, love was simple and enjoyable. The emblem of love was the hibiscus flower, for with its five wide-open petals, its thrusting reproducing parts

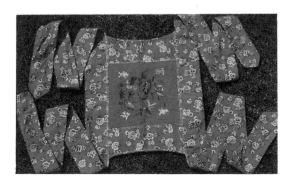

Lucky babycarrier
(Hong Kong)

35

Courting present of
painted jugs. Llanelly,
South Wales, 19th
century

terminating in a burst like an emission, it is love in action. This
symbol is printed for the islanders on imported Japanese cottons,
embroidered by Banaban girls on their ceremonial pillow cases and
stitched into the borders of their palm-leaf sleeping-mats, with
imported Australian wool.

Girls indicate their sentiments by wearing a flower behind their left
or right ear. Banabans of both sexes, right into old age, wear crowns
and wreaths of flowers – and would feel embarrassed without them.
In some Polish villages, similarly, cottages painted blue rather than

Hibiscus love
pattern. Sleeping
mat (Fiji)

white indicate that a marriageable daughter is living there. Prim Victorian misses in England used to manage to convey messages by the manipulation of their fans at balls, and in the language of love *every* flower was credited with a special meaning.

In stable societies it is considered desirable that the begetting of children should not precede the marriage although it did and does by no means infrequently. Outwardly stern and moralist Scotland was notorious for the largest number of bastard births in Europe. Many famous men were born on the wrong side of the blanket – including Keir Hardie and Ramsay MacDonald – and Robert Burns fathered several bastard children by the girls he loved.

One society dressmaker assures me he has made so many wedding dresses for pregnant Scottish aristocratic brides that he

Wedding game, East London children, 1930. (Photograph: Edith Tudor-Hart)

37

evolved a special frontal gathering in his wedding dresses to cover this situation.

The double standard makes life hard for young girls. Traditionally youths are admired for their success with the opposite sex – Don Juans and young bucks are showing their virility. But girls, if they succumbed, lost the respect of the community.

'Now my apron is up to my chin.' She was the loser.

In noble society, where material wealth was not lacking, a different attitude prevailed. Royal bastards were entitled to their own titles and coats of arms where the Bar Sinister carried no shame but something of glory. The 'divinity that doth hedge a king' shines brightly on both sides of the blanket.

Marriage was always, everywhere, a tough business arrangement between the two families. It had everything to do with property – a castle and broad acres, or merely a few goats. The girl and her usefulness was being taken over and the parents had to be compensated. One Catholic priest told me how in the poor rural Ireland of the turn of the century, it was customary at village dances for a marriageable girl, whose father was rich enough to own a cow, to flaunt a smear of cow dung on her white apron to advertise this desirable situation.

Africans, usually so hard on their women, evolved the ingenious system of *lobolo* – a dowry with strings. The bride takes into her marriage certain property – a couple of cows, or a share in a garage, or several goats or a small sum of money. If her husband is unkind to her she has the right to return to her parental home taking her lobolo with her. Since this lobolo will already have been invested, or be calving or in profitable use, it cannot be given back without ruining the husband.

In European countries girls work hard to pile their wedding chest or 'bottom drawer' (sheets, towels, napery, petticoats and stockings). The tough market mammies of West Africa, starting with nothing, may become prostitutes for a while to save up the capital they need to get started in business in the market. They are the principal breadwinners in the family and pride themselves on sending their sons to university in England so that they can graduate to become barristers or politicians or doctors.

The chastity of Spanish virgins, wrote V.S. Pritchett in *A Taxi at the Door* of his observations in the city of Seville, was maintained by the vast numbers of brothels and the thousands of available prostitutes. The most elaborate precautions were taken at meetings in a public park between young respectable people of opposite sexes – an empty chair standing in for the absent duenna. Also, in Italy, when men expect their fiancées to be virgin on marriage, society girls would patronise a surgeon who had perfected the operation of mending the broken hymen for girls who needed his skill. In China and many other countries a bloodstained sheet on the marriage bed was essential to the honour of the bride's family – the lack of it would cause the bride to be sent back in disgrace. Chicken blood was often a handy substitute.

The wedding itself is a very important occasion since, besides uniting two nubile people, it furnishes both families with the opportunity for 'show-off'. A Chinese bride, arrayed in crimson silk, glittering with demon-repellent embroidery and tiny mirrors, was carried to her wedding in a crimson palanquin (poor people could hire one) accompanied by musicians and demon-repelling noises from firecrackers. Red was (and still is) the supremely lucky colour. A courtesan in a brothel is described as having her bed and tables draped with crimson satin curtains and covers. She would get down to business, after playing chess, and entertain her important client with singing, by laying a red silk handkerchief across his knees.*

* *The Scholars*
by Wu Ching Tzu.

Indian and Chinese and Muslim weddings are laden with magic precautions against evil spirits. Since the selection of the partners was a matter for the parents to decide, the bride and groom never saw each other until the time of consummation. Love, as in Indian marriages, was expected to grow as the newly-weds became accustomed to each other and brought up their family.

The Polar Eskimos' dream of a desirable wife was a very plump girl with a circular face and the tiniest possible nose. She might be a bride at the age of twelve, though her husband (who had to be an efficient hunter to keep them in food and fur) would be much older. In a more complex society, a Jewish wedding is celebrated under a canopy wherein the husband smashes a glass under his foot – indicating that the marriage is for life, but perhaps symbolising also the breaking of the hymen.

A white dress for brides is a fairly recent fashion, and in the East of course it is taboo because there white is the colour of mourning. Lord Byron's bride (the unfortunate heiress Miss Milbanke) wore slate-grey satin for her marriage to him in her mother's drawing room.

In a poor Muslim family, a daughter becomes an asset as she becomes nubile, and therefore worth some expenditure on her

39

appearance. In wealthy Muslim weddings it was the custom to display the bride to her husband in a series of dazzling dresses (less wealthy brides borrowed them for the occasion) up to the lucky number of seven.

In one of the *Tales of the Arabian Nights* (Burton's translation) the bride is thus introduced:

> Then the tirewomen took off her veil and displayed her in her first bridal dress which was of scarlet satin and encircled her neck with jewels in the like whereof Iskander rejoiced not, for therein were great jewels such as amazed the wit and dazzled the eye.

This was followed by a yellow, a blue, a green and so on – the seventh outfit daringly made after the fashion of a youth's hunting dress, which audaciously revealed the lovely bride in the guise of a beautiful boy:

> Whereupon she came forward swaying from side to side and coquettishly moving, and indeed she ravished wits and hearts and ensorcelled all eyes with her glances. She shook her sides and swayed her haunches, then put her hand on sword-hilt.

The bridegroom (and the miserably poor listeners to whom these tales were originally told) were getting their money's worth. Burton adds a characteristic footnote about the trouser-cord which held the bride's baggy trousers. It was very important. The tassel could be decorated with the utmost luxury of jewels. Upon the tightness or slackness of this tasseled cord a girl's reputation depended.

Bridal painting on a winnowing tray (Bangladesh)

The rich and powerful Chinese lavished *every* attention on their wedding beds as though they were shrines. They were what we call fourposters, of brilliant red lacquer painted over mahogany and pomelo wood. In winter they were curtained in crimson silk; in summer the curtains were of bright lace. In 1960 I saw such a bed still in use in China. It was like a square room. It had a shelf inside for tea or refreshment. The curtains were of cotton printed with lucky blue birds. This red lacquer bed, however, was in a peasant's cottage deep in the countryside, and the whole family slept in it. In the room there was also a chicken-coop with a broody hen and small chicks scratching about.

* Bracelets and anklets with little gold bells added to the delights of love. There was also the Burmese Bell where marble-sized bells were placed *inside* the lady to make a melodious sound.

One Ming dynasty minister, Ven-Shih-Fan, had his wedding bed (made of Sandalwood and mirrors) able to be rocked by ingenious ropes which caused different sized bells to chime harmoniously when in use.*

A sinister invention (used by outlaw chiefs) was the 'rape chair' which gripped the arms and legs and made prisoner any woman who sat on it, when it collapsed into a bed. This chair was eventually made illegal – the last surviving one was discovered in Szechuan in 1949 and burned.*

* *The Dragon and the Phoenix* by Eric Chou (Michael Joseph, 1971)

But of all the world's weddings none excited so much interest as *royal* weddings, even in Republican countries. Ordinary people love royal weddings – and are prepared to wait in the street all night, whatever the weather, to get a good view of the procession. The reason for this excitement is precisely that magic is involved. The royal wedding is a fertility ceremony. On it mystically depends the fertility and welfare of the people, who are instinctively conscious that the occasion is of the greatest importance. Every detail of the bridal dress is therefore awaited with impatience. Every dress designer in the country designs what he or she would like the royal bride to wear. The making of the wedding dress is an exercise in luck-making and devil-ousting, and every sempstress engaged on the wedding-gown and wedding-train (and Lady Diana Spencer's train was one of the longest ever seen) carefully sews a hair from her own head into the stitching – for luck. On this occasion a young and very lovely girl was marrying the heir to the Throne of Britain and it was miraculously a brilliantly fine day. Surely this augured well for the future of England? In fact, for most people (except that tiny section of the very rich who are unaffected by economic disasters) it got worse. But magic is magic. Everybody loves a wedding and the prolonged joyful pealing of the bells of St Paul's Cathedral was

41

Ganesh with his mother.
(Indian popular print)

doing its job of dispelling the demons.

An Arab caution in a dispute over a future marriage settlement from the time of the Caliph Haroun El Raschid runs: For thou knowest that the masculine is worthier than the feminine and my son is a male and our memory will be preserved by him, not by thy daughter.

More terse is the Arab attitude to women also quoted in a footnote by Richard Burton:

42

Prostitute for pleasure
Concubine for service
Wife for breeding

Burton, however, claims that this originated with a remark of Demosthenes.

We 'liberated', 'educated', 'independent', modern Western women, however, must not become too smug over our advantages. For what does the practical Eastern girl think about the advantages of the Western woman?

In 1962 I was travelling to Delhi in a *Ladies Only* first-class sleeping compartment. The other occupants were a stately Hindu matron and her young western-educated daughter-in-law. They were going to a family wedding several days journey distant, taking with them a huge basket of mangoes. The matron spoke no English but eyed me suspiciously and changed her sari several times during the long night. I thought it was because the carriage was so dusty (the outcaste cleaner's feeble dabs with a broom only stirred up the dust and did nothing to remove it). Now I think she considered that my white female presence was introducing at least a moral caste pollution.

Her pretty vivacious daughter-in-law spoke excellent English.' She courteously offered me a choice of bunks and chattered happily for hours about the Western attitude to women and the Eastern attitude. She had enjoyed the best of both she declared. To equip her adequately for the matrimonial market, she explained, her loving parents had spared no effort. Her horoscope had been cast by the most respected astrologer money could buy – her dowry had included wonderful parures of rubies and diamonds – earrings, bracelets, hand and feet jewels, as well, of course, as a really substantial gift of money.

But these benefits were no longer considered enough. Other affluent families could do as well. The esteemed parental dowry gift for a cherished daughter in India, now, was a degree at an English university – they had chosen the London School of Economics, as she was to marry a businessman. She had enjoyed her L.S.E. studies and duly carried off her degree.

'Of course I realize it's all a lot of rubbish', she assured me, smiling brightly. 'I can help my husband with advice, or indeed could run his business myself if necessary, without the L.S.E. – but that, you must

43

understand, is not the point. It is *fashionable* now for us rich girls to have an English degree.'

At every station her loving husband, and devoted son to her mother-in-law, put his head in at the carriage window to see all was well with them both, especially with his mother. He was a tall handsome fatuous figure, with a beautiful turban and dashing spiv-type moustache, like those adorning the dance-masks of the God Shiva. Beautiful all-powerful male, he was clearly wax in the hands of his obedient womenfolk.

What his young bride really wanted to talk about (as the train slowly moved on again) was the position of Western liberated women, which she regarded as disastrous.

How can they hope to marry properly without an astrologer and without a go-between? How can their parents think of leaving such important decisions to chance? Who is to protect them? They are in a worse position than prostitutes! And think of all those awful divorces – (if they do manage to marry – and many Western women don't marry).

She had heard of London's Matrimonial Computer Bureaux and waved them away – a good astrologer was what was needed, not a piece of machinery. As to one-parent families, she shuddered. A woman's first need, she insisted, was to learn all about men, who, being the Lords of Creation, should and can be carefully manipulated by their loving womenfolk – first of course by their mothers and grandmothers, then by their wives and daughters.

'Their male job is to be the Lords of Creation. Our job, as females, is to keep them content and pull the strings,' she declared, looking as innocent and appealing as a marshmallow.

The ceremonies of The Chinese, who lavish their art on every aspect of life, have
death devoted much skill to the ceremonies of death. Their aim has been to make sure that their dead understand how greatly they are being cosseted, so that not only will their spirits have no cause for resentment (and revenge themselves by causing droughts, floods and earthquakes) but, pleased by the attentions of their relations, actively do them good – from creating bountiful harvests, to ensuring excellent examination marks for the grandchildren.

Fung Shui (the magic science of geographical situation) calls for the services of a good geomancer to indicate the most auspicious site for grandfather's grave. Years before he dies grandfather will have chosen his coffin and made himself comfortable with it. After his death his name goes onto the family tablets so that he is included in the announcements of all family news and worship. On the day of the dead (sacred also in Mexico) grandfather's grave will be swept and adorned by his loving descendants who will spend the day there and share food with his spirit.

Confucius, who advocated concern for life on earth more than concern for the next world, was nevertheless a stickler for funeral ceremonial, which he included in his list of good manners as the mark of a superior man. All people fear their dead and try to appease their spirits, which are easily offended and can become malignant. Have you not seen total strangers on the pavement in England

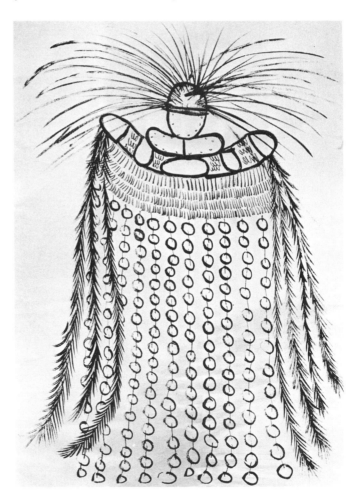

Shell and feather mourning regalia for Tahitian chief. (Lithograph by Pearl Binder, British Museum)

46

solemnly raise their hats when a funeral drives by? Whom are they saluting?

The first Chinese funeral procession I ever saw was in Peking. Huge posters of red and gold, bobbing lanterns, groups of high pole-banners carrying a vertical line of diamond-shaped inscribed flags – no one showing signs of grief – much colour, all-*white* garments (not to Western eyes, of course, the garb of woe). The noise of drums, gongs and fire-crackers was deafening. At first I thought it was a wedding party.

Hindu funerals are marked by the relations circulating the bier anti-clockwise, in order to detach the corpse from life. And the journey to and from the funeral pyre is purposely erratic, to confuse the spirit so it will not return to dwell amongst the living, but accustom itself to continue its endless reincarnations. Everyone wears white. The unfortunate widow (who may be very young, indeed may not yet be a wife except in name) must hereafter wear white and no jewels all her life.

Gypsy funerals are peculiar to themselves and may well be a clue to the origin of these indomitable 'travellers'. The 'wagon' (caravan) of the dead gypsy had to be burned with everything in it including clothes – a heavy loss to the gypsy community. The purpose was to provide the spirit of the deceased with a dwelling, clothes and utensils for its future life. Does this not suggest the Hindu or Zoroastrian or Buddhist funeral pyre?

The practical and thrifty Hong-Kong Chinese common people still provide for the comfort of their dead relations by burning paper cut-outs of money, motor-car, or furniture at the funeral. And Pearl Buck has described the anguished wailing cry of the mother of her newly dead child running in the street holding out his jacket as she tried to recall his spirit back into life. A frequent ritual never lessening in its anguish.

The Polar Eskimos (whose territory of Permafrost is not suited to burial) bury their dead beneath a cairn of stones on the seashore where, dressed in their best clothes (the cleanest and newest fur parka, leggings and fur boots), they go to sit quietly for hours looking out over the frozen sea, meditating and communing with his spirit. Like the Hindus and Chinese, they believe in reincarnation.

The Banabans, now living in the island of Rambi in Fiji (far from their native Ocean Island Banaba, where their honoured dead lie beneath the mined-out craters of the phosphate rock which caused their ruin) have made a new little cemetery on a hillside overlooking

47

Village funeral.
(Wood engraving
by Bewick)

Opposite: Britannia
mourns death of
Lord Beaconsfield.
(*Punch* cartoon)

the Pacific. This is a most moving place – with simple pebble-bordered graves, and a deep silence except for the faint murmur of the sea below and the quiet rustle of tropical palms. The Banabans, too, wear their 'Sunday' dress when they visit there – a clean cotton sulu, a freshly pressed cotton frock, and always crowns and garlands of flowers. They are now devout Methodists – but their concern with nature and their ancestors stems from their pagan past.

James Kirkup reports in *Tropic Temper* that the mourning dress of poor Chinese, settled in Malaya for generations, is a tiny rectangle of black cloth pinned to the left shirt sleeve for a dead mother – while mourning rectangles of cloth for sons, daughters, sisters and brothers are blue or green.

Pious Jews still 'rend their garments' in mourning their dead, as they have done for six thousand years – horizontal or vertical tears, according to the degree of consanguinity.

Of the terrible Plague of 1665 which devastated London, Daniel Defoe wrote 'all the plays and interludes which, after the manner of the French Court, had been set up and began to increase among us,

48

BEACONSFIELD

SWAIN.sc

were forbid to act; the gaming tables, public dancing-rooms and music houses which multiplied and began to debauch the manners of the people, were shut up and suppressed; and the jack-puddings, merry-andrews, puppet-shows, rope dancers and suchlike doings, which had bewitched the poor common people, shut up their shops, finding indeed no trade.' Yet curiously though 'London might well be said to be all in tears, the mourners did not go about the streets indeed, *for nobody put on Black.*'

Manners and Tone of Good Society written by *A Member of the Aristocracy* (11th edition published in 1884) gives precise instructions as to the required periods of mourning by the 'ton', in English society: *A six weeks* for a cousin (*three weeks* for a half-cousin), *three months* for an aunt or uncle, *six months* for sister or brother, *nine months* for grandparents, *two years* for a husband. Sumptuary Laws, which impose limitations on coquetry for widows are especially strict:

> If the bride be a widow she cannot have wedding favours, she cannot have bridesmaids; she cannot wear orange blossoms either as a wreath or on her dress, neither can she wear a veil. She must either wear a bonnet or a hat with veil or tulle or lace as she pleases. And her dress must not be white but of some pale shade of colour . . . It is optional whether a widow removes her first wedding ring or not; but it is more usual not to do so but to wear the second ring over the first wedding ring, the *two* rings on the third finger of the left hand. It would be in very bad taste to wear the first ring on any other finger than on the third finger.

Do we detect here an air of disapproval of second marriages? Queen Victoria had strong views on the subject which she made clear to her devoted subjects. *Widows should never remarry.* However since they sometimes did remarry, 'Member of the Aristocracy' was bound to guide their conduct on the occasion of the ceremony.

At about the same period as 'Member of the Aristocracy' was setting down her rules of behaviour for English climbers into society, the Australian aborigines had just as many rules of behaviour, the observance of which was no less essential and the punishment for non-obedience the same in principle – that is, exclusion from society. Only for the aborigine this was more than a serious set-back – it was a matter of life and death. If an aborigine broke the law of his

Totemic group, even unknowingly, he automatically cast himself out of his group. He no longer 'existed' since he no longer 'belonged'. Then a secretly chosen executioner (always an old man) would proceed secretly to weave for himself a pair of slippers out of emu feathers and hair from his own head. By night he would put on these slippers and quietly approach the sleeping-place of the offending man who, next day, seeing the anonymous marks in the sand of these slippers (which concealed the identity of the executioner, but whose purpose was plain) knew his crime had been discovered and that he was doomed.

Next the pointing of the bone at the culprit (even from far away) was the equivalent of a British judge putting on the 'black cap' – the sentence of death. The culprit had been cast out – he no longer belonged, he was no longer a person, not anybody, nobody. He was dead as a social being, and his body was of no use to him any more. And he proceeded to die – refusing drink, refusing food – doing nothing but slowly dying until he was dead.

The executioner's slippers, having performed their magical task were now of no value – no longer magic, empty of purpose. And they were left lying on the desert sand.

4 *Jewellery*

Don't ever wear artistic jewellery –
it wrecks a woman's reputation.
Colette (Gigi)

I am not superstitious, or am I? I walk calmly under ladders and always look forward to Friday the thirteenth. Yet if I forget to put on a certain pendant when I am dressing in the morning, I feel uneasy all day.

Fertility charm of goddess Ashtaroth. (British Museum)

That pendant is not valuable, nor beautiful. It is a British Museum copy in base metal of Astarte's symbol – an eight-rayed star – a pre-historic clay charm related to her rôle of fertility goddess. It was excavated at Tell El-Ajjul in Palestine and probably dates from 1600BC. One ray is broken.

Astarte or Ashtaroth, as a pagan goddess, was forbidden to the Jews who must have yearned for such a goddess in their dry harsh God-given country. But why has this pendant taken such a grip on

52

me? Against all reason I feel that it protects me (a woman as she is a woman), that it is an amulet which might bring me luck, or if not actually bringing me luck will at least protect me from bad luck. However, just as important as actually wearing my Astarte symbol is the way I put it on. It must be concave side outwards or I feel compelled to turn it round. I know very well that this makes no sense. Perhaps no jewellery makes sense (except to a jewel merchant). But sense is not what jewellery is about, for jewellery goes much deeper than logic, and is deeply rooted in magic.

Jewels are the very oldest element in dress – indeed *are* our first dress, as we can see in ancient Egyptian paintings and sculpture. In India jewels came well before clothes and were and are always much more significant than clothes. Every Indian god and goddess is always portrayed scrupulously attired in full regalia of jewels (protective magic). *Krishna* is sculpted (as Govardhanadhar, twelfth century AD in Halebid) jewelled in an elaborate crown, ear-ornaments, several necklaces, the longest reaching past his knees, breast-girdles, loin-girdles with tasseled pendants, anklets, wrist and upper arm bracelets and shoulder-jewels.

Sacred animals, worshipped as gods, are heavily jewelled wherever jewels can be worn: the sexual regions are always a focus for Indian jewels and I have seen in an Indian museum a jewel-embroidered cover for an elephant's tail. *Nandi*, the sacred bull, is adorned with ear and horn jewels – at least five necklaces of different thicknesses and lengths, leg ornaments and jewels on back and tail (sculpture Chamundi Hill, Mysore, thirteenth century AD). *Apsaras* (celestial nymphs) are sculpted in the Linguraj Temple in Bbubaneshwar (eleventh century) with jewelled crown, ear-ornaments, nose and chin jewels, several twining necklaces, voluptuously curling round and between the breasts, three bracelets spaced on each arm, several loin-girdles with dangling ornaments – one long one passing between the thighs – and leg and ankle bracelets. The evil goddess Kali, consort of Shiva, symbolises her cruelty by her long necklace of human skulls.

To be without jewels is the sign and stigma of the widow. In India every female, of whatever rank and caste, wears jewels – the very poorest must have necklaces, anklets, bracelets, nose-jewels and ear ornaments, even when out working in the fields. She would attract bad luck otherwise. Hands and feet can be magically protected by rings on every toe and the hands caparisoned in a net-work of jewels to which are chained a ring for each finger and

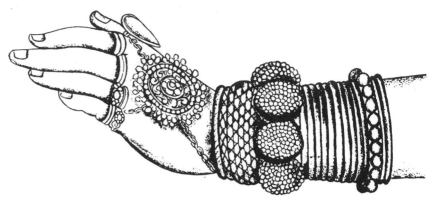

Protective magic hand
and foot jewels (India)

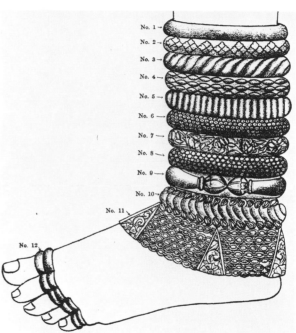

thumb. I remember visiting a desperately poor Hindu family existing in one room in the wilds of the Western Ghats (father, mother, grandmother, many children – and a dwarfed cow, which occupied most of the minute floor). The youngest child, a fierce little boy, was naked except for a bunch of silver fertility charms fastened to his small penis.

Coral and turquoise, so popular in Tibet, are imported from Calcutta, and even the tiniest chips are used in the heavy votive jewellery worn like portable shrines by Tibetan women, especially on holy festival days. The Buddha (according to their ancient

54

Contemporary Indian peasant painting – the goddess Kali. (Author's collection)

records) enshrines in his person *thirty-two signs or symbols*, starting on the sole of his foot and ending with the sacred protuberance on the crown of his head, thus affording comfort and protection to his followers on *every* inch of his sacred body. In Burma and Thailand the Buddha's head is covered with round curls made of lucky turquoises.

In China for thousands of years the most precious of all jewels has been *jade* (nephrite). It is found in a variety of colours and used to be mined in Khotan, in Chinese Turkestan, until the eleventh century but now comes chiefly from Burma.

Jade was esteemed for its qualities of purity and hardness and was extremely costly. In our time the excavated bodies of a provincial Chinese prince and princess were found completely encased in squares of green jade joined together by chains. The jade was believed to confer immortality upon the royal cadavers.

For the funerals of nobles it was customary to close all the orifices of the body with pieces' of precious jade. Jade also connected the emperor of China with the universe and through its magic properties he could communicate with Heaven via a jade disc.

Jade is of course an investment too. Poor Hong Kong women save up to invest in one or two jade bracelets, which for them is not only lucky, but a portable bank as well. The most prized colour of

55

jade is the bright pea green, very expensive indeed – as dear as diamonds of equal size. It is so much prized that a small modern jade-workshop in Peking had, in 1962, coaxed a very old retired jade-carver to return to teach the eager young apprentices. Because he was modest and illiterate, he was reluctant to agree, but they refused to take 'no' for an answer. All they begged of him was just to carry on carving jade whilst the apprentices watched his every movement. A bed and continual tea were provided so that he should not become fatigued.

Confucius himself had the greatest veneration for jade:

> Smooth soft and glossy . . . like benevolence – fine compact and strong like intelligence – angular but not sharp and cutting, like righteousness – hanging down in beads as if it would fall to the ground, like the humility of propriety; when struck yielding a note, clear and prolonged yet terminating abruptly, like music – bright as a brilliant rainbow – like Heaven.

However, there are certain jewels that are believed to be 'unlucky'. Although it does not affect their high value, many people believe this about emeralds. Is it because of their green colour? Possibly, but green is not unlucky in jade. Maybe it is a hangover from the superstitions of the Crusades, green being the colour sacred to the Prophet Mohammed. Others believe emeralds can be associated with arsenic and poisoning. King Henry VIII once bought a costly emerald which turned out to be false. The Tudors used large amounts of jewels sewn on to their Court dresses. No doubt they were not all genuine, even though much treasure was being seized from Spanish treasure-ships returning from the South Americas.

Opals are also often regarded as unlucky, but black opals are particularly highly esteemed by the Japanese, whose agents face the difficult (and often dangerous, for security reasons) journey into the interior of the Central Australian desert to the mining 'town' of Cooper Pedie, where they provide the sole industry.

My own personal preference in jewellery is for inexpensive stones and metals in strong designs – they are full of magic. Arab peasant women, for example, wear a circle of 'coins', each attached to a lucky fish strung on black tape and fastened with a lucky three-cornered tin button. 'Fatima's hand', a popular protective pendant is often reinforced by an 'evil eye' to catch and return evil wishes to the sender. African women wear strong magic necklaces and anklets and bracelets of bones, stones, telegraph wire, ivory, and they always add fertility symbols – cowrie shells. Cowrie shells, which are

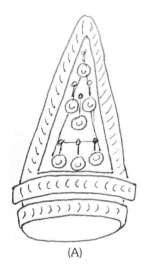

(A)

(B)

(C)

Three symbol rings:
(A)   Prostitute's brass
        ring, Calcutta.
(B)   Seaside souvenir
        ring, Brighton Pier.
(C)   Buddha's tears
        ring. Gold, silver
        and agate,
        contemporary.
        (Author's collection)

in use throughout Africa and often employed as currency are symbolic of female fertility and believed magically to grant riches and protection from danger. I have never seen an African ceremonial or dance dress without them. Entire dance-masks are sometimes composed of close-set cowrie shells. Moreover their fame has spread to other countries. Muslim female jewellery also often includes cowrie shells: while cowrie shells have even penetrated the Polish highlands. The traditional dress of the Polish males of Zakopane (that high region of steep roofs, forests and sheep) includes a shallow wide-brimmed hard felt black hat, with a hat-band of small cowrie shells. Obviously they were introduced for luck, probably by itinerant hawkers. Today they are often found reproduced in plastic.

Because they are easily transportable, jewels have always lured thieves. The famous jewels and treasure of the Moghul emperors in India were seized by Nadir Shah and carried off to Persia in 1739 – it took one hundred labourers fifteen days to melt all the gold and silver and cast it into ingots for easier transportation. Five thousand chests were filled with gold rupees, eight thousand with silver – an inconceivable number of other chests were filled with diamonds, pearls, emeralds and other jewels.

'In a word,' wrote James Hanway, an Englishman who was in Persia in 1744 and especially admired the heavily jewelled horse-furniture, 'the King of Persia carried off treasure from India estimated at 300 chariots of silver rupees, which is the equivalent of 5 billion 400 millions of our silver.' Of the horse furniture he added, 'he had four complete sets, one mounted with pearls, another with rubies, a third with emeralds and the last with diamonds – most of

57

Iranian crown

which were so prodigious a size as hardly to merit belief for many of them appeared as big as a pigeon's egg.'

Certainly the jewels brought the Moghul emperor disaster – nor ultimately did they bring the descendants of his despoiler lasting good either, for the last Shah of Iran had to flee his country without them.

Huge amounts of emeralds, rubies, and sapphires seem to lose all meaning when they are viewed in the mass in bowls and baskets – what can they be used for in such quantity? Persian 'peacock thrones' perhaps or the bejewelled covers for bowls of food which were designed to prevent poisoners attacking the food on its way from the kitchens to the banquetting hall. Another use was found in Moscow when the underground railway was built there in the 1930s – the principal station displayed a large mural map made entirely of precious stones. But essentially it is the cost and the skilled (not necessarily beautiful) setting which makes them marketable. There is an Indian rajah who still keeps baskets of loose pearls as playthings. Once an English lady he was entertaining dug both her hands into one of these baskets of pearls and was horrified to feel a squelchy mess at the bottom. They had 'gone bad' – for pearls are live and they will deteriorate if they are not in constant touch with the warmth of human skin.

Lucky necklaces, Arabia and England

Crystal and pinchbeck
trembling tiara. English,
early 19th century.
(Author's collection)

Jewelled lid to protect
food against poisoners
(Iran)

Since jewellery today is more often valued for its financial worth than for its beauty, most owners of valuable jewels find it prudent to keep them in the bank and wear copies. In the eighteenth century, when highway men infested our roads, lady travellers prudently carried delicate paste jewels instead of real ones. I have such a paste jewel – a very pretty tiara of crystal and pinchbeck, with trembling little circular pendants. Our young designers of jewellery today are increasingly using the simplest natural materials such as pebbles, straw, shells, feathers, bone, or fossils.

Some of the most famous jewels of the past have eventually found their way into the hands of famous courtesans. Empress Eugénie had to flee France when the Third Empire collapsed in 1870, and leave some jewels behind. One of her famous necklaces came into the hands of the well-known courtesan and traitor Païva. Her

Modern Iranian
Imperial tiara

German husband bought it for her as a wedding present. Païva was reputed to wear jewellery worth two million francs. She was banished from France in 1878 for her traitorous activities before and during the Franco-Prussian war. Païva hated the empress bitterly and was delighted to acquire her jewels. There were agents available to buy them for her and her multi-millionaire lover, Count Haenkel Von Donnersmarck, financed the purchase.

A strange sentimental habit of Victorian times was for fiancés and fiancées to wear a tooth of their beloved (carefully preserved after a visit to the dentist) mounted as a tie-pin or set into a brooch. This practice is not different in principle, however, from the Polynesian mourning custom of the widow wearing the skull of her late husband, slung round her neck as a pendant – a practice which startled the white mutineers on Pitcairn Island.

61

The early 1880s were a period when pearl buttons were very popular and very cheap – 4d a gross. Some were of English river pearl shell – more were imported from Japan. At this time the London costers, whose lives were pinched and arduous, were at the mercy of the unpredictable English weather, as well as the all-too-predictable exactions of the money-lenders. Understandably, they depended upon London hospitals for help in sickness and accident. To express their gratitude for this help they rigged themselves up in fancy dress and staged street carnivals on Sundays (their only free day) when they collected money from onlookers for their hospitals which then depended entirely on public donations. Their home-made masquerade dresses used to take the form of Buffalo Bill, or comical cooks and policemen, or stilt-walkers.

Such street carnivals, at this period of lively popular music-halls, were entertaining and noisy. A London street-sweeper (an orphan born in St Pancras workhouse where he was reared and taught to read, write and sew), by name Henry Croft, used to join in the carnivals. But as he was very small and drab (barely five feet – his sweeping-brush was much taller than he was) – he attracted no attention nor, we must presume, donations.

Some of the dashing younger costers (all of whom were extremely vain) began to attract attention by outlining their velvet collars, cuffs, rows of small coat-pockets, and waistcoats with pearl buttons. This gave Henry an idea. He managed to save up and buy for himself a third- or fourth-hand swallowtail dress suit, waistcoat, top hat, cane, gloves and spats, and many thousands of pearl buttons. It is true he did not live from hand to mouth as the costers did. He was an employee of the Somerstown local municipality (earning, at his top salary, ten shillings per week). On the other hand he had Mrs Croft and his twelve children to provide for.

Henry now proceeded to work out his idea. He covered his costume (including boots, spats, cane, gloves and top hat) with his pearl buttons. His next appearance at a Sunday Carnival was a sensation – in a personal triumph, which must have been very sweet to him, he collected more money than anyone else.

Henry's 'smothered' dress was enthusiastically taken up by those costers who could lay hands on enough buttons and could sew. The dress was extremely heavy and difficult to move about in, but its effect was always dazzling. The donations increased gratifyingly.

Henry was a very intelligent man. He resolved next to organize the 'pearly' costers into groups by their London municipalities. Each

The author with Pearly
King and Queen on
Brighton Beach

borough was to have a pearly king and queen (voted democratically
into office by their coster friends). These pearly royalties needed to
declare their regional status, and as the weight of their fully
'smothered' pearly dress had become burdensome, Henry came up
with his second original idea – the declaration of territory on the
back of the pearly costume – in other words *status*.

Before long Henry Croft, himself now Pearly King of Somerstown, St Pancras and soon to consider himself 'Pearly king of all
the world', had organized the election of a pearly king for every

London borough. Each pearly king had his pearly queen and their children ranked as pearly princes and pearly princesses. Besides these, each borough had its 'pearly pride' – four non-royal helpers elected to represent the four wards of each borough. Other pearlies were simply helpers.

The traditional pearly dress of (male) waistcoat, bell-bottomed jacket, bell-bottomed trousers, cloth cap and 'kingsman' (brilliant silk neckerchief) – and (female) tight-waisted full-skirted jacket and tulip-shaped long skirt, white highnecked blouse and enormously wide hat clustering as many coloured ostrich feathers as it could take, was now adapted to its new rank. (Pearly princes wore waistcoat, cap and ruffled shirt, the princesses, a short dress and feathered bonnet.) Usually of dark material, instead of being 'smothered' with pearl buttons like a shimmering mermaid-tail, the back of the Pearly Royal jacket (or waistcoat) was now ornamented with the rank and district of its wearer in bold letters of pearl buttons, for example 'Pearly King of Whitechapel' or 'Pearly Queen of Stepney', spelling out his/her territorial claim and status. The rest of

Pearly royal children, 1910

the costume was now ornamented with patterns and borders of a magic and symbolic nature, showing up strongly on the dark background.

From the start it was a matter of honour and pride for each pearly king and queen to design and sew his or her own pearly outfit – it was not permitted to copy any other because each pearly costume was a personal signature. The resulting costumes were and continue to be a treasury of bold, highly original, witty, beautiful and touching creations.

'*Luck*' of course inspires many of these designs, and patriotism accounts for many more (e.g. lucky playing cards, four-leaved clover, lucky fish, horse shoes, 'old boots', etc.). A cockney passion for London triggers designs of 'Bow Bells' or 'a sailing barge on the Thames by moonlight' (amazingly worked out in pearl buttons, with brown pearl buttons for the brown sails, white buttons for reflection in the Thames and a huge single button for the moon). Some symbols have several concepts – a circular pattern means Big Ben or a pushcart wheel or the sun, for instance.

Certain jackets sport a donkey with a donkey-cart and its owner –

Pearly Queen
Rosie Springfield.
(Collage by
Pearl Binder)

65

some severely geometrical patterns show flowers and 'eyes of God' (diamonds with central dot). There are crowns of all kinds, card suits, crescent moons and stars. In all these costumes the borders are essential and very important. Luck must be enclosed and not allowed to leak out.

Bill Davidson was the old pearly king of West Ham – later New Ham. A very tall, gaunt ex-docker from the years of severe unemployment in the 1920s and 1930s, he fought in both world wars. He never had teeth when I knew him but his huge fists were capable of exquisite workmanship, and his costumes were a miracle of design. His version of Harlequin magic triangles was worked out in very small pearl buttons, which he dyed himself in delicate rainbow colours with packets of Twink.

In 1930 four hundred pearlies followed Henry Croft's bedecked coffin to the cemetery along with three bands, pipers, banners and a film – Pathe-Gazette – photographer. Henry had died, aged sixty-eight, in the workhouse where he was born, having raised a fortune for charity in his spare time, in small coins and through 'lucky' buttons.

Also he had gained status, which is enormously important to pearly royalty. Like most British (especially London) citizens they insist on having it both ways. They are *elected* royal – but their children *inherit* the title.

The Pearlies are a comforting survival. We should cherish them in our increasingly chilly world, for they are artists.

5 *Status*

Red Hat – No drawers
Yorkshire Proverb

Wherever the social order is fixed and stable, as in India, prescribed dress will remain unchanged – sometimes for thousands of years. In ancient Rome one glance was sufficient to determine the trade, rank and district of the wearer – exactly as though he wore uniform.

It *was* possible to rise in society – even slaves could eventually buy their freedom if they could accumulate the money to do so, and in that case altered dress would indicate their new status. But in India caste was (and is) virtually unbreakable. However today the heavy debts of poor Indian peasants can sometimes only be met by the peasant selling his piece of land, in which case he drifts to the nearest town. He is no longer a peasant. His caste is broken. Yet nor is he an outcaste.

In old China each person wore the dress ordained for his situation in life. Down to the minutest detail of dress, his rank was expressed in the colour and shape prescribed for all of his garments – the shape of his hat, the kind of button on his hat, the number and species of feathers permitted to be worn in his hat.

The robes of the emperor of China, for example, portrayed his lofty position as the bearer of the mandate between his subjects and Heaven. It was his duty to be virtuous so as to deserve this mandate. His imperial yellow robes were embroidered with curling clouds and five-clawed dragons (front-facing) of highest status. At the hem of his robes seas and mountains were portrayed, over which his mandate extended. It was believed that virtuous human behaviour could even influence the stars to be propitious.

He possessed different coloured and differently embroidered ceremonial luck-bringing robes in which to carry out his different

67

duties – all in order to ensure the fertility of the soil, the procuring of rain, the prevention of floods, droughts and earthquakes, and the birth of sons. Dynastic princes and dukes and their wives were in their turn allotted their own robes, each precisely embroidered according to rank.

However, the Chinese were well aware that intelligence and character are widely distributed by nature, regardless of rank – and so they introduced a system of examinations, open to all, which led to the very top of the Civil Service. In such a system climbing the ladder to success also involved dealing with other determined aspirants on the way. To keep them down was as tricky as avoiding being kept down yourself by those on higher rungs.

Dress is crucial. 'Sumptuary Laws' in one form or another have been enforced by all peoples, from the most primitive to the most highly civilised, in order to stabilise the status quo in society.

Recorded history of course is always the version of the conqueror. When the Manchu cavalry swept down and conquered China in 1644 they insisted on every Chinese male wearing his hair in a queue (horsetail) to remind them of their humiliation. At the same time they altered all Imperial and official robes – changing the sleeves by introducing cuffs shaped like horse-hooves – to remind the new Manchu rulers that it was by the cavalry they had conquered and that they must never relax or grow soft.

Manchu cavalry
influence on Chinese
court dress

Status   The lesson of this is that you cannot wear what you *like* but what you *must* – unless or until you can reach that higher social grade whose dress you covet. The workings of Sumptuary Laws, indeed, indicate that even among the most primitive of peoples body painting was very strictly regulated indeed. Australian Aborigines, for instance, were only permitted to paint themselves into the grade of their initiation – and initiations with appropriately changing patterns continued into old age. There is also reason to believe that the *size* of a tattoo was crucial among the Polynesians, for they equated size with royalty and their chiefs were all of gigantic physical stature (like the late Queen Salote of Tonga).

To lesser Polynesians large tattoos were taboo. Even today the wearing of the coconut fibre mat, a sign of Samoan royalty, is strictly honoured on important occasions. They are worn in England at royal receptions and garden parties in Buckingham Palace, as well as at home in Samoa.

In tribal Africa native dress and jewellery is very strictly regulated according to age-group and position in the tribe – chiefs and witch-doctors being accorded the most important, most magic dress.

'The Mayor' of Newham.
(Collage by child of 4)

69

* 'The   Squire   en-
deavoured to outshine the
Knight – the Knight the
Baron – the Baron the Earl –
the Earl the King himself in
the richness of his apparel,'
wrote the chronicler, William of Malmesbury, at the
beginning of the fourteenth
century

In the Middle Ages* the dress of every class and group in Europe was most strictly regulated by Sumptuary Laws – with severe penalties if the rules were broken. It was the all-powerful priests who ordained what was permitted. The common people (serfs and servants) wore rough simple home-spun, their feet and legs wrapped and tied in strips of cloth. Shoes of any kind were for them a great luxury. It was the wealthy and noble youths who liked (as what youth does not?) to display their long legs to advantage, and to this end they gradually shortened their tunics, to increasing protestations and threats from the high clergy.

It was a delicate situation, since the nobility were in the highest category, which allowed them great privileges. But the clergy were in the highest category of all and made use of their position to exhort and threaten wearers of 'indecent dress' – but, it must be recorded, without much success.

The 'shamefully short' tunics of the young nobles in the fifteenth century shrank to such brevity, revealing buttocks behind and sexual organs before, both made startling by brilliant-coloured tight hose. The 'codpiece' was then introduced to cover the offending part. This rapidly became a sartorial focus and was worn, even in armour, in a great variety of styles throughout Europe, continuing in exaggerated form into the Renaissance. The region is, after all, of great magic significance; and when the Duke of Norfolk, Earl Marshal and Premier Duke of England, leads the great processions of State he still carries his baton traditionally at the site and in the stance of erection.

The Crusades had introduced into England new foods, new plants, new colours, new armour and the glamorous jewellery and wonderful textiles of the East – we must assume they were looted as prizes of war. English noble ladies seized on these handsome textiles which they made up into sumptuous new fashions. Again the clergy protested – these noble ladies were not behaving like Christians. This time it was not the brevity of the dress that was at fault but the surplus. The great head-dresses – the copious veils (gauze – the transparent new material from Gaza in Palestine), the long full trains, in front as well as at the back, so that – a graceful art – both hands had to be used to lift them, and in general a great superfluity of material: it was unchristian extravagance, the clergy declared when the poor were having to go about half-naked.

So far from the fury of the clergy having an effect on these extravagant Noble fashions – the clergy themselves got carried away

Status　and the bishops and high-ranking church dignitaries began themselves to wear the most sumptuous robes.

As the centuries passed, the rise of the middle class posed a new threat to authority. Money, in large enough quantities, began to overcome the disability of humble birth – especially in England. Queen Elizabeth I well understood the crucial rôle of dress in controlling her subjects (not all of whom had accepted her right to the throne and many of whom were Catholic who looked to Rome and Spain rather than herself). She encouraged young adventurers to explore new lands for treasure – and to intercept and loot Spanish treasure ships on the way back with their booty. The heroes of these adventures were rewarded with knighthoods and lavish incomes (from Monopolies) no matter how humble their birth. As courtiers

Portrait of Queen Elizabeth I. (Gray's Inn Collection)

71

they then became eligible for the highest posts. Their navigational skills eventually ensured the defeat of the Spanish Armada.

This was a period of great extravagance and show-off. At Court the ladies had to be careful not to dress as luxuriously as the Queen, who missed nothing in her surveillance. In particular she sported the huge ruffs invented by the Dutch and sometimes wore two kinds together, the upper one shaped like wings.

Contemporary with the late stages of the codpiece, the ruff (which began in the rich brothels) swept the courts of Europe, developing many fantastic national variations in the process. First it was stiffened with white starch, then coloured starch. (Blue and green starch are both referred to in Ben Jonson's play *Bartholomew Fair*.) A certain Mrs Turner successfully introduced yellow starch into England from France, but this innovation was quickly abandoned when she was hanged for the murder of Sir Thomas Overbury. Bad luck can be infectious.

The moralist Stubbes denounced 'ruffes', protesting at their width of '¼ yarde or more', their starch stiffening and their wanton luxury of gold and silver embroidery. This was also the period of what was popularly known as the 'Bum-Roll', a device tied around the hips to widen the skirt and at the same time make the waist look smaller. Robert Crowley wrote in 1550 in his *One and thirty Epigrammes*:

> A Bumbe like a barrell
> With Whoppes at the skirte
> Hyr shoes of such stuffe
> That may touce no dirte
> Her mydlle braced in
> As small as a wande
> And some by wastes of wyre . . .

Even the Queen herself, gorgeously dressed and made up, did not escape comment:

> . . .
> Fair hair such heddresse
> Being as nature could not have produced . . .

But the bum-roll, the wired corset and the unnatural blonde hair had been invented because the status-seeking men liked women who were wide-hipped, big-buttocked and blonde. And eventually their own wives adopted these brothel fashions.

Ruffs, in fact, had needed careful regulation. Elizabeth's sumptuary laws included the severest penalties for exceeding what was permitted – especially in the provinces where trouble might begin at any time. So the Queen posted inspectors armed with large scissors at the gates of London to measure the ruffs of all who passed in or out. Any ruffs exceeding the permitted size were cut down on the spot.

The situation changed again with the accession of James I. He (who had seen much murder) was so terrified of assassination 'by the stilete' that he held up the normal development of male fashion. The male breeches, which were beginning to lengthen and narrow, he arrested by having pumpkin-shaped huge heavily padded breeches (if they can be so called) specially designed for him for the protection of several vital parts of his body. (He was a believer in magic and witches.) The Court had to follow suit.

King Charles II was so determined to enjoy his nearly lost heritage and the lovely women and excitements now available to him, that dressing up to his rôle of monarch bored him. He wanted to be comfortable in his dress – and his mistresses to be readily available.

The dress of the Court ladies in the famous Lely portraits of his

City dinner. (Collage by Pearl Binder)

73

reign look like night attire – very loose, very soft, slipping off in all directions. There is also one portrait he had painted of Nell Gwynne in the nude – but somehow it is not voluptuous at all nor does it reveal her as well put together: undersized, short in the leg, a rather pale pathetic little Welsh girl – one cannot guess her smile nor her wit from this portrait.

As to dress, Charles II, that symbol of unabashed sexuality, decreed and wore the long-buttoned coat from which present male coats are descended. The male wig he accepted – hair (even someone else's) being a strong magic sexual symbol, whether he knew it or not. He was always short of money and prepared to sell almost anything to acquire enough for his considerable needs – even state secrets to spies (of whom one was his mistress). But he knew that status in dress can be achieved either by *extravagance* – for example the *Royalists* in the Civil War with their floating curls, ribbons, laces, rich materials, wide-topped boots, such as the popular Prince Rupert – or by the exact opposite, by restraint. Cromwell's followers were severely dressed in their plain black cloth garments – cropped hair (not too cropped, however, lest it look like polled catholic priests), white linen collars and plain riding boots. It is the winning side which sets the fashion.

The Quakers were Puritans, of course, but their non-conformity to Cromwell's ideas (they were totally against fighting) angered him. Many Quakers spent years in jail for having ideas of their own and acting on them. George Fox, the shepherd mystic who pioneered the Quakers, disliked the 'unmanly' ribbons, wigs, laces and satins of the fashions of his time. He also abhorred the dirt that clung to them. The dress that he evolved was of puritanical simplicity, suitable for a hard life – often in jail – and much travelling. It consisted of leather breeches, a plain coat, knitted plain hose, strong shoes, plain shirt, plain linen collar. The linen had to be scrupulously clean. The female Quakers wore the simplest gathered gown, wide linen collar and linen cap. Quaker dress became (unintentionally) a *status dress* because of what it avoided.

The growth of British trade, manufacture, and expanding colonies made (some) Britons very wealthy in the next hundred years – despite the set-backs of the breakaway American colonies and the Napoleonic wars. Tradesmen, if rich enough, might now aspire to Society. But unless they were really very rich indeed, they had to be kept in their place.

Manners and Tone of Good Society (1884) describes those

74

entitled to enter 'the charmed circle of fashionable society' which ensured them 'a position in the social scale otherwise unattainable':

The families of the aristocracy, the families of the country gentry, persons belonging to either the military or naval professions, the Bar, the clerical, medical and other professions, the families of merchant Bankers, and members of the stock exchange *and persons engaged in commerce on a large scale* . . .

The English middle class in Paris, 19th century. (du Maurier drawing)

But at trade, *known as retail trade*, however extensive *its operations, the line is drawn*, and very strictly so, as were a person actually engaged in trade to obtain a presentation, his presentation would be cancelled as soon as the Lord Chamberlain were made aware of the nature of his occupation.

Nevertheless:

> But the sons and daughters of the wealthy manufacturers, are not *themselves* debarred from attending drawing rooms, and levées if their wealth, education and associations warrant them in so doing.

Was the aristocracy still smarting from Napoleon's gibe that the British were 'a nation of shopkeepers'? *Retail* was the unforgivable word. If you were in *wholesale* or had made really enormous sums of money (and this was a great period for selling adulterated food such as sanded sugar, watered milk, or arsenic-tinted sweets) you were no longer a tradesman but a 'Merchant Prince'. The locked door *could* open. As the author of *Manners and Tone of Good Society* continues:

> It is imperative for ladies to wear 'evening dress' when attending 'drawing-rooms', that is to say low bodices and short sleeves, and trains to their dresses, which trains must not be less than three yards in length . . .

Gin-sodden children
from London's East End,
19th century.
(Gavarni lithograph)

76

Status   It is compulsory for both married and unmarried ladies to wear plumes. The married lady's Court plume consists of *three* white feathers, and the unmarried ladies of *two* white feathers; and a lady must either wear lace lappets or a tulle veil.

The wearing of low bodices is absolute though, under very exceptional circumstances, permission can be obtained from the Lord Chamberlain for modification of this decree: if the application be accompanied by a certificate from a physician as to the inability of the applicant to appear in a low bodice.

Queen Victoria's court was not very entertaining, all in all. Prince Edward used to escape to Paris whenever he could find an excuse, to romp with the demi-monde, with whom he was so popular that many years later an old boulevardier sighed, *Of the old lot only the Prince of Wales remains. And he went to the bad. He became a King.*

In another quarter of a century King Edward, now safely on the throne, was cultivating rich 'merchant princes' like Thomas Lipton, who sold tea in large quantities (retail, mind you) and whom in due course he knighted. By then American heiresses (no matter how their papas had made their money) were marrying into the British aristocracy and so were not a few of the gorgeous chorus-girls (from the London slums mostly) in the popular Daly's musical comedies. Bernard Shaw declared these imputs of fresh blood saved not a few ancient noble lines from decay and collapse.

The sons of such successful manufacturers had to be sent to private schools to be turned in to 'gentlemen'. During the 1939-45 war I took a one-day-a-week job teaching 'Art' to the boys of an evacuated prep school from Surrey. I did my best to interest them in the joys of line and colour but all they really cared to draw were Spitfires and Messerschmidts. Once I managed to persuade them to try another subject – 'A Picnic'.

Every single one of the boys drew a detailed picture of an enormous car drawn up beside a busy motor-way, with the boy's fashionably-dressed family sitting on fancy folding chairs on the narrow grass verge, about to tackle the lavish contents of the immense food-hamper with an assortment of matched cutlery, fancy china, smart table napkins, costly giant thermos flasks and an array of bottles of wine spirits and liqueurs. I felt sorry for these poor little rich boys and mentioned their idea of a picnic to the Headmaster.

77

Unemployed in
Hyde Park, 1930

'What do you expect?' he said scornfully. 'Young Jenkins' father actually manufactures lavatory seats!'

The headmaster felt the slur bitterly. He had no time for 'Art' either, assuring me he would never have included it in his syllabus except that the boys' parents expected it. But, as I thought it over, it dawned on me that the headmaster himself knew no Greek or Latin – his talent was to sell his own out-of-date concept of a 'gentleman' to his clients, who should have seen through him but, since they were in trade, it was he who made *them* feel ashamed.

A friend of mine (a gifted musician born into poverty) was brought up in a slum street in South London. Their terrace house cost five shillings and sixpence a week to rent. The terrace houses on the other side of the narrow street, even smaller, cost only four shillings and sixpence a week to rent. My friend's mother absolutely forbade him playing with the children living on the other side of the street, whom she despised as common, vulgar failures.

In my experience social class is the crucial status factor in marriage, transcending even colour. Not long ago a wedding was celebrated in Grays Inn. The bride-groom, son of an English Judge, was the regulation blond young English barrister – a sound Conservative, educated at all the right schools, thinking all the right thoughts of his class.

78

HAPPY THOUGHT! LET US ALL HAVE A VOICE IN THE MATTER.

Noble Breeder of Shorthorns. "WELL, YOU ARE A SPLENDID FELLOW, AND NO MISTAKE!"
Prize Bull. "SO WOULD YOU BE, MY LORD, IF YOU COULD ONLY HAVE CHOSEN YOUR PA AND MA AS CAREFULLY AND JUDICIOUSLY AS YOU CHOSE MINE!"

'Breeding'. *Punch* cartoon, 19th century

The bride, also a barrister, was an ebony-black girl from Nigeria, daughter of a Nigerian Judge. The parents of the bride and bride-groom – so black, so white – were like contrasting piano keys. All were beautifully dressed in conventional formal wedding attire (virtually unchanged since that diligent 'member of the aristocracy' wrote her authoritative book of rules on exactly what should be worn, a century ago:-) The bridal gown, the bouquet, the lordly male morning-dress, the carnation button-holes, the absolutely regulation smart silk dresses and conventional smart hats of the two mothers, the conventional floral decoration of Gray's Inn Chapel, the conventional clustering society and press photographers on the steps outside the Chapel – all was safe, secure, predictable. A Judge's son was marrying another Judge's daughter, what could be more suitable, more desirable? But what an uproar there would have been, what storms, pleadings, tears, angry changing of wills, cuttings-off, there would have been had the young English barrister wished to marry a white girl from the wrong social class.

Status? What is it? A magic fiction dependent on time, place, people, dress – disarrange one domino and everything crashes. What is important, what keeps people going and keeps tribes and nations going is to know who they are.

The pecking order in the farm yard is a fact of nature. In tribal

79

society it hardens into rigid law, enforced by many taboos, especially sartorial taboos. What you may and may not wear are crucial in tribal life, and equally crucial in the tribal life of modern society.

Reception at Buckingham Palace. (Drawing by Pearl Binder)

6 Decline and Revival of Tribal & National Dress

* Local dress

Adieu Foulard*, Adieu Madras*
Adieu Chaine d'Or*, Adieu Collier Chou*

Doudou a moi
Y'a k'apparti
Hélas! Hélas!
C'est pour toujours
Hélas! Hélas!
C'est pour toujours

Bonjour Monsieur le Capitaine
Bonjour Monsieur le Commandant
Moi k'a fait un 'tit petition
Pour laisser doudou a moi ba moins
Moi, k'a fait
Un 'tit petition
Pour laisser doudou a moi ba moins

Mais mademoiselle c'est bien trop tard
La consigne est déja signé
Doudou à vous
Y'a k'apparti
Hélas! Hélas!
C'est pour toujours
Doudou à vous
Y'a k'apparti
Hélas! Hélas!
Y'a k'apparti
Hélas! Hélas!
C'est pour toujours!

Folk Song in Patois from Martinique The girl is trying in vain
to get her lover released from the ship taking him away for
good – conscripted for Napoleon's wars

West Africa. (Silk screen print by Dan Jones)

Tribes are held together by the strongest laws and magic taboos, the purpose of which is to protect the tribe from its enemies and bind it together to ensure its survival. Successful tribes expand and, by enlarging their territory, extend their hunting and food-gathering possibilities. Some tribes evolve no further than this, their territories being unsuited to anything but totemic nomad life. The Australian aborigines exemplify this.

The next stage of evolution is when a tribe begins herding, settles in one area and gradually starts farming. Villages grow up which could develop into towns. Towns can become cities and cities eventually become the basis of nations. Such evolution is necessarily of very slow growth, and any attempt to hurry up the process can lead to disaster and conflict. For instance, when oil was discovered in Alaska the life of the Polar Eskimos became drastically altered.

Peter Freuchen wrote in the 1950s: 'Their daily needs made it imperative for them to be at the right time just where they could find the animals necessary for their survival . . . and which they could only get from certain animals – but at the same time they had to go inland to get reindeer's skin and the sinews they used for thread. They needed walrus skins and sealskins but they also had to fish for salmon in the lakes. On the tiny islands far out at sea they found their birds and eggs.'

The Eskimo traded furs and fish for the goods they wanted from the Hudson Bay Company. Hunting and fishing being their way of life that was fine. But Freuchen has nothing but hatred for 'free traders' who introduced such amenities and then stopped coming to trade, leaving the Eskimos worse off than before – for what good is a rifle without bullets?

Eskimo ingenuity was such that they could make sledges, 'the ancient way in these treeless regions', from rolled-up reindeer skins frozen into the required shapes, or large salmon frozen into crossbars. When missionaries came, there were quarrels between missionaries and traders who had diametrically opposed plans for the Eskimos. Then, in Alaska there were first the gold fields – then fisheries, sealing, and later American military and naval bases along with the discovery of oil, and the building of the Distant Early Warning radar chains (D.E.W.). Tinned American food is now flown in, nylon clothing supplants fur clothing, and the grand-children of Eskimo hunters never learn to fish. What will happen to them when the oil runs out, as run out it eventually must?

Arctic Eskimo female
dress
(A)   Traditional
(B)   Modern

During the Soviet drive to industrialise their backward country in the 1930s prizes were awarded to workers who distinguished themselves in learning and applying these new industrial techniques. One such worker, from a nomad tribe beyond the Steppes, was given a fine new town flat with parquet floors, central heating, electric light, and, to columns of praise in the press, moved in with his wife.

She could not take it. Accustomed to living in a tent in the open and cooking on a camp fire, she cried for days at her unhappy promotion. At last her husband returned from work one day to find her happy again. She had pitched their old tent in the middle of the beautiful living-room, lit a nice smokey fire of sticks on the parquet floor in the middle of the tent, put on her former skin and fur dress and boots, and regained her serenity and her old personality.

All over the world the same conflict develops, as the white man's ways are introduced into regions where they are alien. It is the older native people who understand best what they are losing, and why the wonderful new white man's amenities seem to be killing off the native recipients.

Just as the Australian aborigine had developed what he needed to live in his desert, so other peoples in different countries evolved their own laws, own magics, own taboos and their own clothes – suitable for those countries and conditioned by them. For while well-meaning white missionaries imposed their alien religions on natives who were deeply and devoutly religious in their own ways, the trader usually followed close on the missionary, who had introduced the white man's ideas of sin. As one example – in the Polynesian tropical islands the missionaries decreed that, as the naked body was 'sinful', every child as soon as it could stand upright must wear loin covering – preferably imported cotton shorts or skirt – or at least a covering of imported cotton. In the Fiji Islands, however, this adamantine law broke down on some of the remoter islands where even punishment for its disobedience did not work. They simply could not afford the cotton. The girls continued to wear their home-made skirts of strips of palm leaves and their children ran about naked as before, trying to keep out of sight of the infuriated missionary.

The Maoris of New Zealand were similarly christianized. In his travel book *Our New Zealand Cousins*, published in 1887, the Hon. James Inglis writes:

The old native dress is giving way to the perhaps less graceful habillements of modern civilization. The men affect English fashions, not only in boots, ties, coats and dress generally, but in the cut of their whiskers and their fondness for billiards, horse-racing, whiskey and other so-called luxuries. A tall belltopper surmounting a grizzly tattooed visage is quite a common sight in Auckland or Napier.

James Inglis was a Scottish clergyman and pursued his enquiries steadily.

'Do you think the adoption of European dress has an injurious effect on the health of the Maoris?' we asked (of Captain Blair who commanded the Arawa contingent of natives during the war). 'Undoubtedly – especially when they adopt some of the more insane devices to cramp and distort the human frame – high-heeled shoes for example.'

Chief Tuteao Manihera declared,

In the days of our ancestors the natives mostly died of old age. When they slept at night they used fire to keep them warm and in the day they basked in the sun, its heat serving them as clothing – and the people never died off. But the arrival of the Europeans to these islands brought disease amongst them and two complaints made their appearance, namely chest complaints and cough. From that time the number of natives began to decline. Subsequently another disease called 'measles' and now fever has come and rheumatism. The food and clothing are now very good but the Maoris are dying off rapidly.

Across the world the American Indians were faring even worse:- Speaking to General Grant's American mission in 1875 (after his people had been imprisoned before being sent to a reservation), *Chief Joseph of the Nez Percé tribe* declared:

The white men were many and we were few and we could not hold our own with them. We were like deer. They were like grizzly bears. Fighting, always retreating before the white invaders' superior weapons and larger numbers, we were doomed. We had a small country. Their country was large. *We were content to let things remain as the great spirit made them. They were not . . .* and would change the rivers if they did not suit them.

85

Indian chiefs in manacles being sent to Washington. (Drawing by George Catlin)

Chief Joseph's father *Tu E Ḳakas* who died in 1871 warned his son:

> Always remember that your father never sold his country. A few years more and white men will be all around you. They have their eyes on this land. My son, never forget my dying words. This country holds your father's body. Never sell the bones of your father and mother.

Today (some one hundred years later) what is their situation? In the Idaho reservation 28% are unemployed. There is discrimination in job-getting. There is lack of educational skills which could give the young men pride. They are taught to 'think white' in order to succeed. But it does not work that way. They simply lose their own language and their own traditions.

The Red Indians could learn from white men when it made sense to them. The horse, for instance, was not indigenous in America – the Spaniard invaders had introduced it in the sixteenth century. Some horses escaped and bred on the great prairies whence the red Indians caught them and learned to use them. Yet the Nez Percé Indians, a tribe of famous horse-breeders had kept peace with white men for more than fifty years.

Even in the 1980s the same process was being witnessed in the

86

missionising of the Panare Indians of Brazil by an American fundamentalist sect 'which uses threats of everlasting punishment, destroys native customs and beliefs and all tribal ceremonies to make them dependent on imported consumer goods. (Both sexes of Panare wore woven loin-cloths of blue and white beads). They were strong and healthy and could run or walk fifty miles a day. Within a year these people had learned to hate their former way of life – sang hymns – wore dirty western cast-off dress. The end of the road is drunkenness and prostitution. They do not live long, having nothing worth living for.' *(Sunday Times Magazine, 15 May 1983)*

Yet, ironically, oppression from without can be responsible for the revival of native and village dress. The glamorised Scottish tartans and splendid full male Scottish dress were the answer to their battles with the English attacking their identity and their land. Today tartans are a flourishing industry, beloved by exiles with Scottish names and eagerly sifted over by Italian designers for new ideas. Queen Victoria's sentimental affection for the Scottish highlands dressed English middle-class little boys in kilts for two generations.

The gallant Poles, invaded for centuries by Swedes, Germans and Russians, forbidden to speak Polish in what remained of Poland, reacted by cherishing and insisting on their distinctive Polish village dress being worn in each district – so that today nineteenth century Polish village costumes are the best researched, the best made and the best worn of any. Their little village churches joined in the fight to preserve distinctive Polish dress-identity – the priests refusing to marry village couples unless they wore their native village dress. Today when so many countries support their travelling dance-groups to display their national culture, the Polish folk-dance groups are outstanding – moreover the dancers *are village dancers* (given a final polish by professionals). And all this stems from *the nineteenth century* – when throughout Europe folk dress was disappearing under the assaults of industrialisation. There is even a Polish *city* folk dress – that of 'cobblers' sweethearts', their nineteenth-century boots being audaciously laced with brightly-coloured long shoe-laces.

Folk-singing and folk-dancing belong together, for folk-dress is the festival and ceremonial dress worn only for festivities – dresses of great value on which are lavishly skilled and gorgeous embroidery, sometimes gold and silver, lace, costly ribbons, beautiful cloth and fine linen. Such dresses (male and female) are heirlooms carefully kept to be handed down in the family for many generations.

87

Mexican woman.
(Drawing by Dan Jones)

The rich variety of Mexican village dress survives by reason of its very deep pagan roots, mixed for centuries with ideas from the invading Spaniards. These Mexican dresses display much magic symbolism – the very weaving involving ancient fertility rituals and the looms themselves having male and female parts.

Old fertility pagan magic even survived in advanced industrial countries. When Cecil Sharp began researching into disappearing English and British folk-songs, he either did not understand, or, much more likely, deemed it prudent not to reveal, the pagan and sexual nature of most of them. 'Down Yonder Green Valley', for instance, is not a sentimental love-tryst; nor does 'Buttercups and Daisies' mean just picking innocent wild flowers. Sharp's folk-songs were laundered for the middle classes, who were growing sentimental about the disappearance of the rural England of their dreams: hearty yokels in clean smocks dancing around 'innocent' maypoles whilst their plump cosy wives naively tressed corn dollies (which middle-class English ladies have since taken up themselves as a 'craft').

The truth was harsher (as Benjamin Disraeli records in 1845 in his novel *Sybil*): English farm labourers, underpaid, half-starved, and at the mercy of the big landowners, plotted in desperation the burning of ricks; the Tolpuddle martyrs were hanged or transported to Van Diemen's Land for daring to form an 'association'. Nevertheless the old fertility pagan magic was not entirely crushed, the delight undiminished in curious and ingenious skills with the materials available to poor farm labourers (straw, wood, etc.). Horse-brasses were magic in design and protective in intention, as magic-protective as the blue beads which Arabs fasten on their camels and donkeys and now dangle on the screens of their taxis.

Agricultural depression ruined many small British farms and drove the farmers and labourers into the towns. The handloom weavers (proud of their skill) and the lace-makers (masters of their craft) were dispossessed by the clanking new machines. Illiterate, they lamented their condition and sufferings in poignant songs which survive and have been collected by Ewen McColl. Negro workers' songs have been collected by Alan Lomax, and sailors' shanties and the songs of 'transported' prisoners by Bert Lloyd. These are a far cry from Cecil Sharp's laundered folk songs; they are bitter despairing laments and conscious historic recordings as are the songs of the transported 'felons' (on their way to Australia and Van Dieman's Land) in the nineteenth century.

In 1976 the American bi-centennial celebrations featured the International 'Folklore' Festival held on the green banks of the Potomac river. England was represented by a group of Yorkshire Morris-dancers, and also by a pearly queen (Rosie Springfield). The idea behind this festival was to invite village dance groups from the old world to meet the descendants of immigrants from the same countries of the old world.

Peasants emigrate in hope of a better life on more productive soil, with less harsh landlords – and it is the young who emigrate. One folk-dance village group came from Portugal – poor middle-aged peasants, thin, gnarled and dignified. Their festival dress, handed down in the family for generations, was magnificent – richly embroidered velvet jackets and bodices, shirts and blouses of fine linen trimmed with strong hand-made lace, handsome embroidered felt breeches, swirling multi-coloured felt skirts over lace-trimmed hand-sewn fine linen petticoats and actually *leather* shoes, polished to dazzling brightness. Their stockings were of white thread, hand-knitted in entrancing designs, each pair different. Their dances

89

were strong, intricate and traditional – some going back centuries to record episodes in Portuguese history.

Their American hosts were descendants of Portuguese emigrants from the same villages. A century of American progress had produced big strong blond teenagers, University fodder, who had carefully learned for this occasion their ancestral Portuguese folk-dances. They all wore tee-shirts and crumpled shorts or tee-shirts and old blue jeans, with clumsy canvas shoes. It was impossible to guess they were from the same race as the Portuguese dancers.

Afterwards I asked the tee-shirt dancers why they had not dressed in the Portuguese festival costumes, expecting to be told they would be too expensive and too difficult to make. Not at all. They all agreed they would feel foolish dressed like that.

Yet people, *all* people, love display. They may hate the office of High Court Judge or King or Field-Marshal, but they appreciate the elaborate eye-catching dress that goes with the job. In the same way, people of all countries feel on firmer ground when their nation is symbolised by an accepted symbolic figure, who is symbolically dressed. They need such magic symbols of themselves:

John Bull
* Instead of John Bull we now have Mrs Thatcher. Tories see her as Britannia. Socialists see her as the destructive demoness Kali wearing a necklace of skulls.

(the middle-aged comfortable early nineteenth-century squire-farmer, dressed in tailed coat and waistcoat over his comfortable belly, and topboots) pronouncing his sound British opinion on every political crisis anywhere in the world. Early *Punch* cartoons show him with less belly and even stronger opinions.*

Uncle Sam

(bearded and not at all young – his tall stringy figure togged up in stars-and-stripes tail-coat, long ill-fitting trousers) looks like an energetic travelling salesman or the folksong tin-kettle mender. He has not changed his image at all, though everything about him has.

Marianne

(the heroic classic female figure – mother of brave sons, revolutions and the Centre Pompidou in Paris) wrapped in windswept marble draperies revealing much of her breasts, and carrying her flaming torch (of civilization, or, insurrection? No doubt both) on pedestals all over France. But that is the old-style Marianne of the history books. Today (and for the past century at least) Marianne is the pert lively country farmer's wife – young, arms akimbo, dressed in a high-crested bonnet (like a wave about to topple), tight bodice, short full skirt, sturdy bare legs and sabots. Every bit as patriotic as her

John Bull and Uncle Sam.
Punch cartoon, 19th century

A CRUMB OF COMFORT.

earlier incarnation, she stands up today for Camembert cheese and the demands of French farmers in the E.E.C.

At the end of the second world war James Laver and I were commissioned to prepare an article predicting the line fashion would take in the post-war years. We in England had done without fashion throughout the war. Most women had been in uniform of one kind or another; and clothes were still severely rationed. Our patriotic slogan was 'make-do-and-mend!' I was, as we discussed the article, wearing an old tweed suit of my husband's, ingeniously scissored down to my size, the four-panelled skirt cut from the trousers.

Laver and I began by looking towards France. Where had the ordinary French woman got to in the war years? What shape had she evolved for herself out of the bitterness and turmoil? Dior was in the future. Sartorially she was still on her own.

We started researching into French photographs, drawings, cuttings from French war-time newspapers, even gossip. When I assembled all this together and drew it, a clear outline sprang into life. The ordinary Frenchwoman had turned the pre-war tight-waisted bodice, short full dirndl skirt, clumpy shoes and overhanging high shovel hat, into what? 'Marianne!' Consciously or unconsciously, she was France's answer to the Nazi occupation.

The Russian bear represents the Soviet Union, as it represented Tzarist Russia. In *Punch* cartoons throughout the nineteenth century it is huge, avaricious, clumsy, barging into Middle East, Turkish and Chinese problems, and sniffing avidly at the borders of Tibet and Afghanistan – always wearing the Russian peasant's peaked cap. A far cry from the useful stuffed bear in the entrance halls of the big Russian hotels, where it serves as hat stand, and even further from the twee Soviet emblematic bear produced for the Olympic games in Moscow in 1980.

The Chinese national symbol is undoubtedly the unfailing ancient fertility-sign of *Yin-Yang* – the curving double basis of creation, each curve indispensable to the other, and applicable to both crops and humans. The Dragon is recognised and accepted everywhere in China as the rain-giver, but the Yin-Yang is basic – unchanged and unchanging for thousands of years.

Such national symbols need no words, need no national anthem, and include *all* their nationals, not just those who are momentarily in power. Today there are tribes, and even nations, driven from their own territories and countries, who in exile still hold together – even when hopelessly scattered: the Jews who have a religion and written language count their history back six thousand-odd years; the gypsies, perpetual nomads, and now other refugees from war and invasion – such as the Boat people. What holds these apparently uprooted rootless people together? Religion perhaps?

Between East and West sartorial exchanges have always created problems. When the Japanese decided to enter the Western world towards the end of the nineteenth century, they were advised to send to the most renowned tailors in Savile Row for correct attire for their first meeting with western bankers and industrialists. When the strange Western garments arrived they were carefully examined. Top hat, shining black shoes, swallow-tail coat, lapelled waistcoat, wing collar, discreet tie . . . but the 'flies' in the trousers foxed them. For what conceivable purpose was this strange opening?

After much anxious deliberation they decided that this opening could only be intended for the rear. When the momentous East-West meeting took place the Japanese were dressed in every respect like English gentlemen, except that they were all wearing their trousers front to back. The story was, of course, hushed up lest the Japanese loss of face destroy the delicate, new entente.

7 *Religious Dress*

When the missionaries arrived, the Africans had the land and the missionaries had the bible. They taught us to pray with our eyes closed. When we opened them they had the land and we had the bible.

Jomo Kenyatta
1978

A child's drawing of God

Witch doctor, shaman, village curate, Buddhist priest, Hindu guru, Obeah woman, right up to the lofty altitudes of Archbishop of Canterbury, Hebrew High Priest and the Dalai Lama – all religions are served by their Holy men and all Holy men must wear distinctive Holy garments which embody magic. For religion is concerned with the supernatural and its interpreters must wear magic.

Witch doctors (usually hereditary, sons learning from fathers) are consulted when ill-health or misfortune strikes. Africans believe disease and misfortune are caused by enemy spells. The job of the witch doctor (dramatised by manipulation of bones, pebbles, or claws) is to discover the enemy spell-caster and force him to remove the spell, under threat of receiving a worse one.

In drought-ridden Africa and all dry countries the rainmaker is equally important. Rainmakers are weather forecasters who profess to induce rain. They have expert knowledge of cloud formations and ready explanations of counter-magic spells if their promises of rain misfire. Their official garb, both as witch doctors and rainmakers differs from the garb of their clients by the bird-wings, animal claws, snakeskins, and little magic bags hung about them and the powerful magic rattle which they use.

George Catlin's painting of the Plain Indian Blackfoot witch doctor Wun-Nes-Tow, depicts him covered by a huge, snarling-headed, grizzly-bearskin, and hung about with snake-skins, animal bones, beads and fringes of human hair.

Blackfoot medicine man

Siberian Shaman

Shamans (who were active in Siberia and the Arctic), claimed to be in close touch with the world of spirits and able to transmit messages from them. Shamans drummed and whirled themselves into fits and trances during which they 'visited the realms beyond'. One Siberian Shaman regalia for such visits was made entirely of bird-feathers (birds are universal messengers between this world and the next). Another is made out of animal hide with a deep heavy fringe and a tall pointed rough hat of fur. The Shaman drum is all-important. Made from a sacred tree and the skin of a consecrated animal, it transmits the Shaman's magic power into the rhythmic sound which will summon the spirits to receive him when he magically reaches them.

The polar Eskimo Shaman Sordaq, whom Peter Freuchen knew

so well – and who jovially decried his own magic Shaman powers, perhaps from Eskimo good manners – conducted his séance stark naked, his limbs bound in sealskin thongs cutting into his muscles, drum and drumstick beside him and also a piece of dried sealskin, and all the blubber lamps extinguished except for one tiny flame.

Presently the drum banged, and the sealskin rattled loudly from all directions. Freuchen seized Sordaq's arms to feel if he was making the noise. They were still bound tightly. Sordaq was 'attempting a journey to the underworld to try to find the reason' why there had been so many strange accidents and tragedies in the settlement for the past year.

After the terrible din stopped the blubber lights were put on. Sordaq had disappeared. The Eskimos attending the séance were writhing and swaying – one had a seizure, 'howling like a wolf' . . . Then they all 'began to shout in a language I didn't understand. It was not the usual Eskimo language but they all seemed to understand it'. Presently Sordaq returned. 'Again his drum made the igloo tremble and the crackling sealskin flew through the air.'

Sordaq then announced his message from the underworld. 'The great spirits are embarrassed by the presence of white men amongst us. Three deaths are still to come – our women must refrain from eating of the female walrus until the winter darkness returns'. Sordaq, Peter Frechen says, was sitting on the ledge, tightly strapped in his sealskin thongs. He was obviously exhausted.

Aztec worshippers in a fire ceremony

Noise is an indispensable part of religious ceremonies (except for the silent Quakers); bells, clappers, hand-clapping, rattles, especially drums, are all used to frighten off lurking evil spirits in every pagan gathering, and in Christian gatherings too, for church bells are, in truth, rung to warn off the devil who has harmful intentions at weddings, funerals and christenings.

Hindu India, the oldest continuing civilization in the world is steeped in magic beliefs. It is the land of a myriad religions, a thousand strange deities with multiple heads, legs and arms to show their power – often animal-headed – or human-headed holy animals. They have the gift too of changing themselves into mountains, rivers, giants, or dwarfs. Hindu Priests wear either white voluminous garments or hardly anything, according to the sect of the particular God they worship. All wear the sacred thread and all wear the insignia of their God painted on their foreheads.

Buddhist priests in hot countries wear a simple draped saffron robe and go barefoot.

Tibetan Buddhist lamas wear heavy robes of Yak wool, for the high altitudes of Tibet produce bitter winters. The colour of these robes varies with the sect of their monastery – dark yellow is the colour of the leading 'gelugpa' of the four sects, and maroon is common.

The Dalai Lama (now in exile in India) had an extensive wardrobe of magnificent magic robes, each for a particular ceremonial occasion in the Buddhist-Tibetan year – one was for the demon-expulsion ceremony danced to the sound of the very long booming 'Alpine' horns. The Dalai Lama's very large ears are an essential part of his holy persona (and must be considered as part of his magic dress). The people believe the original Buddha had huge ears to enable him to hear the world's woes.*

* It is the ear-lobes which are the focal point – being very long. The magic is thus reinforced by the obvious penis symbol of immense power.

There has always been much influence on Buddhist ceremonial dress from adjacent China – particularly in the richness of materials, and the shape of boots. For the Emperor of China's special mandate to act as 'go-between' connecting – in his person and by his moral behaviour – Heaven and Earth, he wore Imperial robes heavily embroidered to explain and illustrate this. His long wide-sleeved yellow silk robe was embroidered* at the bottom with symbols of mountains and rivers. The front of his robe was embroidered with golden front-facing five-clawed dragons, symbols of his lofty rank. Only members of the Imperial family had the right to wear the

* This Imperial dress was as much a symbol of status (Chapter 5) as it is of the Emperor's religious significance.

98

dragon insignia but only the emperor could wear front-facing dragons.

Symbols of small curly lucky clouds – for rainbearing and magic fertility – were embroidered all over his Imperial robe. All exits of his robes (hems, sleeve-ends, neck opening) were heavily reinforced by demon-repulsing, luck-inviting embroidered borders.

Amongst the many Imperial head-dresses (worn with his various costumes, each for a different ceremony, to ensure the well-being of his vast dominions) was a square silk tile (like a mortar-board) having pendant curtains of 288 bead-jewels suspended from the sides facing front and back. This was to enable the emperor – should he by chance encounter a displeasing unlucky sight which might incur his anger or distress – to lower his head and shut out the unpleasant

Bead fringe head-dress
to hide unpleasant sights,
Imperial China

object. For it was essential for the emperor to maintain his tranquillity and not endanger the vital link between earth and heaven.

Confucianism, which held China together through two thousand years, was not a religion, rather a system of ethical behaviour and good government. Confucius himself believed in the good example, and filial piety. He declared, 'Why ask me about the next world? Let us make life bearable first in this one.' His pupils reported his rules on dress thus:

In undress   Confucius never wore anything red.
In warm weather   a single black garment over an inner garment.
In cold weather   a black garment over lamb's wool. Over fawn fur a white garment, over fox fur a yellow garment.
At home   a long fur dress *(fox or badger)* with short right sleeve – *his sleeping robe* half as long again as his body.
Underwear   (except in ceremonial dress) silk cut narrow above and wide below.
Visits of condolence   neither black cap nor lamb's fur.
Fasting dress   linen, exceptionally clean and bright. He always liked everything to be ship-shape and orderly.
He put on Court dress   when the villagers were exorcising pestilential influences.
The superior man,   he said, 'does not use deep purple or puce colour in his dress-ornaments'.

His precept included:

'Let every attainment in what is good be firmly grasped.'
'Let relaxation and enjoyment be found in the polite arts.'

There is still Confucian influence in present-day Chinese life: tact, politeness, filial piety, a love of peace, a nostalgia for traditional behaviour, all of which have survived the destructive years of the Cultural Revolution. Politeness and good government are never to be sneezed at.

The magic inherent in religious dress spreads out beyond its confines, announcing divinity, as in the halo, or beckoning inviting-ly, as in the Hindu Kolem and the Haitian Vevers.

The Hindu Kolem is a magic symmetrical diagram inscribed at the entrance to a dwelling and at the eating-place of each member of the

Religious Dress

(A) Vever of Goddess
     Erzulie
(B) Vever of Seagod
(C) Vever of drums of
     God Ogadon
(D) Catholic/Pagan
     Vever
drawn by Voodoo priest
in ashes on ground to
summon desired gods
(Haiti)

(A)

(B)

(C)

(D)

family or guest-house. It is sifted on to the floor in rice-gruel or coloured powder(s), usually by a servant girl who cannot read or write, working rapidly and joyfully, taking immense care, because only the very best is good enough for the Gods and her Kolem is for that special purpose.

A Kolem is an altar to a particular god or goddess, an invitation to come and occupy it, to be adored, and to help the family. Kolems need to be interpreted, for they can be very complex. There are no less than sixty-four classic Kolem motifs – all having astrological significance (e.g. snakes mean sex, the lotus purity, the fish – riches). Each angle of each part of the Kolem represents one degree of the power of the planets and their influence on man. Care is needed, for a downward line signifies destruction (a knife), and must be capped like a fencing foil to contain its dangerous power.

In Haiti the urgencies are fiercer, more urgent, more desperate than in China. *Vevers (or Vévés) are* the sacred symbols calling the desired God from the underworld to serve the worshipper. They are drawn on the dark ground with maize-flour or ashes by the Voudoun (Voodoo) priest. The plates of flour or ashes for drawing the Vevers (or symbols) are first signalled towards the cardinal points – to the chanting of 'Fait un Vever pou moin' ('draw a Vever for me'). The drawing of the Vevers requires great technical skill and is an essential part of the training of a Voudoun priest. A small amount of flour is picked up between thumb and forefinger and sifted onto the dark ground into the required lines – radiating around the sacred Poteau-Mitan, the centre post avenue by which the loa (recalled spirit) is brought to the séance. Each loa has his special Vever – *crossroads for legba* – serpents for Damballah – boat for Agive – heart for Erzulie.

During the ceremonies which follow, these elaborate Vever drawings are destroyed (the offerings of grain, or the blood of chicken-sacrifices being walked and danced on). Finally the Vever is swept away when traces of the séance are cleared up.

Relentless drumming from the Voodoo priest or priestess, always dressed in white (the death-colour)* may well be not so much coaxing as *forcing* the spirit deity to come and occupy the Vever and then take over ('mount') the body of the supplicant to ensure his needs will be met (money, curing of disease, or return of faithless lover, for example). The supplicant (an impoverished peasant who has scraped and saved to afford this séance), tottering under the weight of the loa who is 'riding him', speaks with the god's voice. In a

* The dress has changed. Hesketh Pritchard reported a century ago 'for covering the Mamaloi wore a thin white robe, tied with a red sash and a string of gold in coloured beads – in full dress the Papaloi's piece-meal vestments are red, the sacred colour'.
'Where Black Rules White' H. Hesketh Pritchard, FRGS, Thomas Nelson & Sons.

102

word he is 'possessed'. (The Hebrews also had such a concept, called a *golem*).

Voodoo is the religion of the hopelessly poor Haiti peasant. It is a bloodcurdling mixture of ancient African magic rituals and noble concepts (from Dahomey, Nigeria, Senegal, and Ashanti) brought to Haiti by slaves, joined by Caribbean natives, American Indians, negro escapees from the Southern cotton-fields, and peppered with Roman Catholic religious ideas. *The purpose is always to bring back the dead to serve the living.*

The loas are distinctive, having strong personalities and eccentricities. They include *Legba*, the phallic male-female God of market-places and especially of crossroads. He guards the divine gateway to the next world. He is the black night of death and always wears black – an old man, always hungry, leaning deceptively on a stick, for he is immensely strong. He mocks at passion. He is keeper of cemetaries – it amuses him to appear unsummoned to interfere and spoil ceremonies, dressed in dreadful rags and a little perky multi-coloured cap. However, he loves children and is doctor and patron to sick children.

Damballah (the good serpent in the sky) the ancient venerable father – his home is in water. All supplicants ask of him is his blessing, for he is the origin of life and the rainbow is his mate.

Agive, Sovereign God of the seas is offered banquets (long saved up for) on a sailboat at sea. He is one accredited lover of the beautiful tragic Goddess *Erzulie* and the nuptial bed their devotees prepare for them is twelve feet by eight feet – covered with fine linen, two lace-edged pillows (one corner of the sheet turned down as in a good hotel), a bouquet of roses as offering, and a perfect

Stephen Gardner,
Bishop of Winchester.
(Gray's Inn Collection)

conch shell (used as the call for Agive). He is the guardian of sailors and all oceans, real and spiritual.

Erzulie, tragic goddess of love, is identified with the Virgin Mary, and also with the erotic dreams of all men. She moves in beauty swathed in luxury of every kind, elegant, perfumed – every girl's dream of herself – also promiscuous, successful, rich. Yet, at the moment of triumph Erzulie will weep tragic tears for herself and for all women – for love has failed her. Her 'toilette' is kept in readiness, the best a poor Voodoo chapel can buy – an enamel basin (unchipped, unstained) for her ablutions, the water steeped in basil for she insists on total and absolute cleanliness – new soap still in its paper wrapper, several embroidered towels, comb mirror and toothbrush, a fresh white or pink silk handkerchief, perfume – a dress of white or rose fine linen with lace trimming and (because she loves jewellery) several necklaces of gold and pearls, earrings, bracelets and three wedding-rings. She never neglects supplicants who are devoted to her, she loves to dance, and she rewards handsome men.

The forbidding of Polynesian pagan dancing by missionaries was disastrous both to the natives and to their white invaders. What took over was pruriency in the invaders, boredom and loss of will to live in the natives. Dancing was their religion, their response to their natural environment – their joy in life; a rich language of pagan affinity with nature. The Polynesian girl dancers wore a kilt of stranded tanned palm-leaves exposing the navel – anklets and bracelets of pure white seashells. Crowns and garlands of fresh flowers perfumed their dancing. Their breasts were bare. The mékés of fingers, hands, hips and knees were their interpretations of the waves of the sea – the leaves fluttering on the trees – an emerging butterfly opening and closing its wings. It was sexual, as nature in

Sunday morning in Suva, Fiji. (Lithograph by Pearl Binder)

104

movement is sexual. It was 'yes' to life. The missionaries were offering 'no' to life.

In Hawaii the missionaries worked hard to make the native women hide their 'sinful' luscious bodies in 'Mother Hubbards' – the big high-necked garment like a loose nightgown. When they succeeded, the native women, barefooted and unused to any such covering, wore nothing underneath and carried themselves so that the Mother Hubbards revealed every line of their bodies even more than without them.

One curious result of the Mother Hubbard has been that the tourist shops in Hawaii now all stock large numbers of them – in the gayest colours – they are snapped up by English and American matrons off their cruise-ship for a few hours. These matrons put them on over their corsets and wear them with high heels and an artificial plastic flower in their blue-rinsed hair.

Today in Fiji every Sunday morning in Suva you will see a solemn procession of Fiji families making their way to the methodist church where they will sing Moody and Sankey hymns in five-part-time with glorious voices. Wearing their Mother Hubbards, carrying their 'Baibara' (bible) in one hand and a plaited straw fan in the other, their husbands in decent Sulus (longer on Sunday), choking white shirts and neckties, and their young children itching in stiffly-starched frocks and tight suits, all wearing crippling shoes of stiff patent leather they cannot afford. It is to show their respectability and their earnest desire to be as rich as the white man. Meanwhile, in the expensive tourist hotels other white men are lounging round the swimming pool in the briefest of cache-sexe – their girl friends wearing very little more – attended by handsome young Fijian waiters, dressed (because the tourists demand it) in a wisp of bright Sulu patterned with suggestive hibiscus and wearing a real hibiscus behind one ear.

The Hebrew High Priest, as described by the Roman Jewish historian Josephus, wore the sacred dress of the High Priest or Chief Rabbi of the Hebrews in which he worshipped at the Temple which Solomon built. It was distinguished by strong magic-protective tribal symbols. The underdress of pure fine white linen, the blue over-dress, tied with a girdle of multihued embroideries, were of the finest, most carefully woven materials – to be worthy of their invisible all-powerful God and Protector Jehovah. The breastplate displayed twelve precious stones – one for each of the tribes of Israel:

105

Traditional vestment of
Hebrew High Priest
of Jerusalem.
(Reconstruction by
Barbara Phillipson)

Reuben	– Red	Dan	– Sapphire
Levi	– White, black and red	Ged	– Grey
Judah	– Azure	Napthali	– Rose
Isaachar	– Black	Asher	– Beryl
Zebulun	– White	Joseph	– Black
		Benjamin	– 12 colours

The two shoulder brooches of sardonyx were engraved with the
names in Hebrew of the sons of Jacob, six on each stone. The
forehead was covered by a gold plate bearing the name GOD.

King Solomon himself used to employ magic and he wrote a
famous handbook on its usage. Josephus stated that the Hebrew
vestments represented:

linen	– the earth
cap of blue	– Heavens, the sky
bells	– thunder
ephod	– the four elements of the universe
gold	– the splendour of enlightenment
breastplate	– the world centre
girdle	– the ocean

106

Religious Dress	*Two shoulder jewels (sardonyxes)*	– sun and moon
	Crown of Gold	– the splendour which pleases God
	Twelve stones	– the twelve months and signs of the zodiac including

Emerald	– spring
Ruby	– summer
Sapphire	– autumn (truth, sincerity, constancy and chastity)
Diamond	– winter, the sun, light

The Jews incorporate these attributes into their twelve tribes. The hem of the blue overdress displayed a magic-protective border of bells and pomegranates – bells to stop evil spirits, pomegranates to promote the fertility of the twelve tribes. The headdress was of fine gold. The feet were bare – so that nothing impure should enter this sacred place.

The temple being regarded by the Jews as their powerhouse of spiritual strength, its windows were designed with frames widening outwards so that the holy power generated inside might benefit faithful Jews outside.

The early Christians, poor and simple followers of a new faith, wore the simple working dress of their calling – fishermen, shepherd, and the like. Christ himself, a carpenter, would have worn the heavy apron of his profession. The tradition that Christ was red-haired may well have some foundation – for there are still a considerable number of Jews with red hair and light eyes.

The Muslims, dedicated to Islam, the Prophet Mahomed and his Koran, followed the Old Testament but only up to a point. They even acknowledge Christ, but only as a minor prophet. A tribal people of the great deserts of the Middle East, their skills have always been in trading, whether in camels, carpets or oil – and a passion for fighting.

The geometrical fixation of Arab art (which at its Moghul peak produced superb architecture, carpets, gardens and jewellery) is due to a misunderstanding of the Biblical veto on 'graven images'. This means 'no graven images *of God*' – that is to say, *no making of idols*. However the blocking of one channel often leads to amazing developments in another. The austerities of the Islamic faith (and their religious leaders are robed with extreme austerity) found one outlet in the Jehad – their holy war of expansion which brought them almost into France; and in Spain there are still Islamic houses, with splendid Islamic tiles, throughout Catholic Spain, as far as Cadaqués, and a theme of Mexican folk dances and religious face-masks as well as Sicilian puppet-shows, is still Moors versus Christians.

The Islamic assault on what is now Indonesia has brought Islam to almost all this string of Islands, excepting Bali which remains devoted to Hinduism. Islam has had a strong influence on traditional Batik patterns which, animals or flowers not being allowed, ingeniously display concealed wings (of the Garuda Bird) or small parts of flowers in their riddle patterns.

Java batik

The Polish city of Krakow, invaded by Islamic Turks, put up a famous fight and still retains their captured tents. These are very large and luxurious, made of beautiful chintzes, lined and padded like rich ladies' drawing-rooms – a far cry from the harsh little Bedu tents of black goat-hair where the Islamic religion first took hold. They reflect the luxuries of Baghdad.

108

Religious Dress Muslim women must piously shroud themselves out-of-doors – some of their 'veils', notably the 'Burqua' – a total shroud of heavy black horsehair which excludes light, air and vision – are still worn by devout Islamic women. These were common in Uzbekistan in the 1930s, and when the Soviet government encouraged the women to burn them in a great bonfire on the Registan Square the infuriated mullahs attacked and killed not a few of these 'advanced' women. One was even burned to death by mullahs with ignited petrol for removing her Burqua in public.

Christianity and the rigid splendours of Byzantium, whence derives the Greek Orthodox sect of Christianity, robes its priests in gorgeous stiff vestments and rich crowns, whose shapes echo the golden cupolas of their cathedrals. To the Protestant western world this seems a far cry from Christianity, especially the great painted faces of unforgiving Saints staring down from the ceilings of Greek orthodox Russian Cathedrals, to terrify the congregation.

In the Roman Catholic church papal vestments reflect the pope's awesome authority and at the same time display many magic pagan symbols. For instance the gaping top 'fish-head' of the popular papal crown is a great deal older than Christianity. It is a phallic,

The yellow star of condemnation, Nazi Germany and Poland, 1939

109

life-renewing symbol associated with all lunar deities, once worshipped in Assyria and Ancient Egypt, still sacred to the Hindu Gods Vishnu and Abuna, and also revered by Buddhists as well as being the emblem of the Jewish Passover which is celebrated in the month of Adar the fish.

Pope Innocent III (1198–1216), who thought as highly of the Torah as he greatly detested the Jews, instituted the segregating compulsory yellow star (sometimes also a horned hat) which triggered off many of the terrible pogroms which disfigured civic life in Europe for so many centuries (one feature of these pogroms was the traditional seizing of the goods and chattels of the Jewish victim). Hitler revived it in Nazi Germany and this racism culminated in the horrors of the extermination camps of Treblinka, Belsen, Auschwitz – and others, wherein not only Jews but Poles, gypsies, and active opponents of Hitler in captured countries, were also exterminated.

To this day the Poles are faithful to the traditions of their Roman Catholic religion – delighting in its mysteries, miracles and festivals, worshipping their Black Madonna 'Queen of Poland' – and keeping up their gingerbread sculpture and the one-inch high galloping horsemen and barking dogs of baked dough for Saints' Days, as well as their traditional High Tatras paintings on glass.

The freedom from the rule of Rome which England achieved under Henry VIII, went to the heads of the English like strong wine – resulting in a multiplicity of religious sects – some with a political

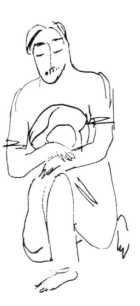

Mexican peasant on
pilgrimage

110

bias, others mystic. The Puritans became the most powerful of these sects – for the most part middle-class English farmers and solid merchants, they lacked humour, dreaded witches, and wore black with broad white collar and plain cuffs. Their women wore a white cap beneath their tall, wide-brimmed hat, and white apron. Work-obsessed, the Puritans stopped amusements and games and burned many paintings belonging to royalists because they regarded them as wanton and obscene.

Sundays to the Puritan meant attending church all day. Some devout Puritans wore handwritten verses from the Bible next to their skin. The jewellery of this period reveals their obsession with death and the macabre – skeletons and death-heads' mourning rings predominate. Those Puritans who emigrated to America took their terrors, obsessions and mania for hard work with them. It is still there, especially in corners of New England.

At last, however, the common English people rose up against the joyless life the Puritans were giving them, and by the nineteenth century the protestants had settled down, in classic English fashion, to a class-division: High church for the aristocracy, Low church for the shopkeeper, no church at all for the independent-minded but, instead, chapels where the minister was kept firmly in his place by the congregation. This was the pattern when English missionaries were most active abroad, and numerous.

In my childhood in Staffordshire in the early twentieth century church-going was a serious business – a class exercise if ever there was one. The *poor* children, who wore black clogs during the week (made of wood to measure by cobblers – turned up at the toes and held together with their polished leather uppers by tiny 'brads'), wore special brown clogs for Sunday – and the brads were tiny brass-headed nails. Very smart they looked and very good for the feet. With these went corduroy trousers reaching below the knee, a starched white blouse with sometimes a wide collar.

Middle-class boys wore highly polished leather boots, Norfolk jackets and Eton collars or, daringly, sailor suits and round hats with turned-up brims and the name of an imaginary ship on the ribbon. If there was no fighting it was because they went to different places of worship – the middle-class boots went to church – the working class clogs went to Chapel.

Filled with unshakable belief in themselves, their white God and their own superiority, though rarely well educated, the missionaries took themselves and their severe wives off to India, Africa, the

Polynesian Islands, and Australia. Sometimes, coming from modest homes, it was their only chance of feeling themselves superior to other people, even though they were heathens. For some energetic Englishwomen (like Mary Kingsley) it was their one chance to get away from a suffocating domestic life and see something of the world.

Daisy Bates was herself an Anglican, but her relations with the aborigine were a very unusual combination of sympathy and insight. Certain aristocratic, very high-church missionaries preferred the harsh labours of the Solomon Islands, determined in their own words to treat all natives 'like old Etonians'.

Wherever the missionaries went they found the natives already ardently practising religions of their own, pagan, un-English, but suited to them and their own environment. The more ignorant the missionaries were, the more intolerant, the more harm they did. And there were so many sects of Protestants – each sending its own missionary. In Africa the natives soon learned to go from one sect to another to collect gifts (bribes?) of blankets, sugar, and second-hand clothing to cover their naked children.

What most upset the missionaries (with their black boots, black umbrellas, harmoniums, stiff collars, highnecked blouses, long skirts and pince nez) was the lack of shame, lack of all sense of sin on the part of the natives of tropical climates. The girls went naked above the waist. The men wore a leaf loincloth The children wore nothing at all.

They gladly learned the hymns (inaccurately translated, for most were untranslatable) and sang them loudly with flourishes of their own – and showed great curiosity and astonishment at the missionaries' dress – at his domestic paraphernalia. Dr Livingstone's

Gypsies on the move
in Central Europe.
(17th century engraving)

112

African converts were amazed at his trousers, for which they could find no logical or magical reason whatever – they were uncomfortable and made running impossible. They had taboos of their own but they could never understand what upset the missionaries so much about the naked (or half-naked) human body. However, the black velvet neck-ribbon, a sign of Victorian gentility introduced by the lady missionaries, has now become part of the native costume of the Banabans.

When a snail loses its shell it is finished. How then do nations survive who have lost their native country? Poor wanderers, can they hope to be accepted by another country if they are a different colour, speak an alien language, *dress differently* and worst of all have no money?

The 'Boat People' refugees from North Vietnam toss about the China Seas in unseaworthy boats for which they have been charged far too much, not knowing where to go, what to do. Nobody wants them.

What then of the big immigrations – of people forced out of their native land (for everyone starts somewhere) with nowhere to go to and nothing to take with them. How do they survive? What holds them together? How do they dress?

Let us take two peoples – one nomad the other city-oriented – the Gypsies and the Jews. While it is possible that the gypsies came from Northern India – perhaps as outcastes – now they are found in every country in Europe, most numerous in Romania where, from the fifteenth century onwards, they made excellent needles for the monasteries and churches engaged in church embroidery. They are still there, always poor, always nomad, but they have kept

religiously to their own strict observances about weddings and funeral rites and the cleanliness of their cooking and eating utensils even when only tin cans. They do not like their women 'marrying out' and look with disfavour on the fruit of such unions.

Horses are not a means now for them to make a living. The men trade in small lots of this and that – sometimes old motorcars. Gypsies have always liked metal. Their women still tell fortunes, sell 'lucky' sprigs of heather or lavender, make and sell clothes-pegs and buy odds and ends of second-hand-clothes to wear (blouses and bright full cotton skirts preferably) and cheap glittery jewellery. The men wear caps, mufflers, old flannel shirts, corduroy trousers – mostly second-hand. They look like country tramps – perhaps out of defiance.

The Jews face a different problem. They are not by nature nomadic – 'the wandering Jew' is not wandering; he has been dispossessed and is on his way somewhere else. The Jews have the advantage (and pain) of a very strong ancient religion with strict rules of observance, a written language and two spoken ones. Their dietary laws are extremely strict.

Jewish families, when they get a chance of settling somewhere, adopt the dress of that country as they adopt other peoples' food (except meat): their soups and pastas are Italian, for example, and their sweets near-Eastern. They love clothes and their girls (as

Poor Moroccan Jewish immigrants. (Lithograph by Pearl Binder)

Anatole France pointed out) can be very beautiful. It is a meritorious act for a Jew to encourage his wife to dress well and be beautiful for him. The 'Sheitle' (the wig which a pious Jewish woman adopts on marriage) is *not* a penance – it is (I was assured by a devout Rabbi) to enhance their beauty. She may have several and keep them all in fine trim.

The praying apparel for Jewish men is the hat (always kept on in Synagogue – or else a small cap), the voluminous praying-shawl (of white silk with fringed border and blue or black horizontal stripes near the ends). Their women pray upstairs, segregated. Students of the Yeshiva (training to be Rabbis) dress in the style of the 1880s in Europe – black felt hats with a large brim, sober black suit (summer and winter) beard and 'peyes', traditional side-curls which have been worn for thousands of years and can even be seen in Egyptian mural paintings of Jewish prisoners.

The ancient Hebrew prophets used to warn the Jews against addiction to pride and arrogance, and against flamboyant dress, lavish living, showing-off. But humility does not come easily to the Jews. The 'home-coming' Jews from Europe have little in common amongst each other except their ancient faith. They have absorbed the cultures or lack of culture, of the countries of their exile. The most truly Jewish are perhaps the Yemenites, shepherds from ancient Yemen, still speaking Biblical Hebrew. Yemenite men wear gowns, Yemenite women wear trousers. The slight, slim Yemenite women carry everything on their heads (even a can of tinned tomatoes). Their songs and dances, their bubbling yodels of pleasure, come from the Far East. The Yemenite father makes his daughters' beautiful dowry jewels himself with only the crudest tools, each jewel different.

Here we must put in a word about the common man, the faithful attender at church, the Buddhist peasant who gives from his own scanty meal more than he can spare into the priest's begging bowl, or the wretched low-caste Hindu townee, desperate for help.

I once saw an extraordinary ceremony. I was walking through a night market in Bombay – hoping vainly for a breath of air after a torrid day. Through an open window in an adjacent house came a loud ringing of bells. I peered in. The suburban sitting-room was crammed with worshippers. There was an enormous vulgar pink plastic effigy of an elephant. Facing the worshippers were six tall men, dressed in spotless white shirts and trousers, like cricketers. Each was ringing a heavy handbell, directed by a man in ordinary

115

Hindu dress. I thought this semi-private puja must be in honour of Ganesha, the elephant gift-bestower. Beside me, outside the window, a very poor thin man was praying desperately, his skinny arms raised towards the sound of the clanging bells. I have never seen such frantic entreaty. He believed so passionately in the power of that pink plastic toy to bring him succour if it cared to. He needed something so badly he was trying to catch a whiff of kindness from the plastic gift-giver, to which he was not entitled. Caste too low? Maybe an out-caste. No money at all, obviously. Was it an urgent debt? A daughter to be married and nothing for a dowry? A sick child? I never found out.

It is rewarding to travel, as I always did, on small old cargo ships in far waters. The poor people are travelling because they must – jobless, not wanted – not of the right race – but desperately hopeful. Such a family was the McDonalds, going to Australia. Father, a short wiry logger from the forests of Burma (half Burmese but proud of his Scottish name); mother, big, quiet and silent, a full Burmese; six tall fine sons in best white duck suits and a beautiful daughter, Evangeline, eighteen, dressed in a plain white dress. Every night she played Moodey and Sankey hymns on her old harmonium, which they all sang to earnestly.

'You see we don't fit in any more,' explained Mr McDonald sadly (whilst little Sikh boys, with their hair-nobs tied in lucky green parcels, romped all over the salon). 'We are too British for the Burmese and too Burmese for the British. Our family have lived in the Burmese forests as loggers for generations. We are Methodists. Now the Burmese don't want us. We are going to try our luck in Australia, if we can get in'.

'What will you do, Mr McDonald?'

'Oh Miss, I think I might try my hand at catering . . . I've had no experience but perhaps I may be lucky . . . We must trust in God . . . And every night we pray it will all work out alright . . . The boys are fine loggers . . . do you know if there are any forests in Australia?'

Indigo print of the
Resurrection for a duvet
cover (Czechoslovakia)

116

8 *War Dress – Peace Dress – Protest Dress*

We have guided missiles
And misguided men
Martin Luther King

Scarecrow. (Wood engraving by Bewick)

The purpose of military dress has traditionally been to display courage and to frighten the enemy. War being a male exercise in the display of power, the impression created by grandiose military dress usually counts far more than its practical use in battle. For instance, in the Middle Ages the armour of noblemen (going to the Crusades

118

or merely to tournaments) grew so heavy and elaborate that it was more dangerous to the wearer than protective. Apart from its great prize-value to the enemy, the difficulty of mounting a horse in full armour, and the impossibility of remounting if dislodged made it impossible. On the other hand, the visor offered fine opportunities for frightening the enemy with terrifying face-masks. Japanese armour in particular excelled in this.

The Civil War in England was a class war. It was eventually won by the more efficient army – that of the Roundheads – whose soldiers were clad very plainly but serviceably. Cromwell's troops were the up-coming sober middle-class. The Royalists or Cavaliers, the aristocracy, wore their fashionable but unserviceable attire of wide-brimmed felt hats with floating feathers over long curled wigs. Their coats and leg-covering were adorned by fancy braiding, clusters of loose ribbons and much rich lace. The gauntlets of their riding boots were so wide and loose as to be a positive hindrance in action. Often they were filled with lace ruffles. The Royalists also wore large flowing capes. Altogether not a good fighting dress, especially in contrast to the Cromwellian uniform with its accoutrements of steel helmets, tall lethal pikes, and breastplates.

The war dress of the American Indians of the Plains (those whose proved valour entitled them to it) included the magnificent 'war bonnet', – a crown of eagles' feathers sweeping to the ground, each feather embroidered at its peak with a small twisted red feather, to keep the lucky power from escaping. The warrior was hung about with scalp trophies, fringes of human hair and necklaces of grizzly bear claws besides bow, arrows and spear. His horse also was adorned, even sometimes crowned, with similar eagles' feathers.

Mounted Crow chief

119

Deerskin leg-coverings left the buttocks bare – a practical custom. (Was this the origin of the extremely tight seat which persists in the cut of American trousers to this day?) The warrior's hands were left free for firing arrows or using his spear. But how *could* he fight, encumbered by his huge war-bonnet?

The Crow warrior chief 'Long Hair' (according to George Catlin) grew his hair to the length of 10 feet 7 inches, and wore it folded around a leather strap into a block 12 inches long which he carried under his arm. Hair being a universal symbol of masculine valour, this advertised his virility. But did it affect his physical adroitness in battle?

The Japanese were masters of the art of frightening the enemy. Just as they had moulded scarifying face-masks on their visors, it was reported as late as the Russo-Japanese war (1905) by the *Illustrated London News*, that the uniforms of ordinary Japanese soldiers included a fox tail protruding from the rear of the trousers. This was supposed to give them the supernatural magic power of the fox spirit, a demon well known to Japanese and Chinese peasants. If the enemy understood, that would be a bonus.

Napoleon believed devoutly in luck, and used to encourage his successful generals to design their own uniforms. The result was a tribute to the power of male fantasy. The generals adorned themselves with height-giving, shoulder-widening, 'fancy dress' borrowed variously from birds, Africans, the Comédie Francaise and classical Rome. High brass helmets with ostrich feathers, epaulettes of gold with quivering metal fringes, vivid colours of coat and displayed lining, high-braided collars, broad sashes, magnificent sword belts and swords – high-heeled glazed thigh boots, panther skins, leopard skins: how many of these glories, one wonders, vanished in the snow during the retreat from Moscow?

Napoleon was more practical when equipping his Navy. He ordered all his fighting ships' decks to be painted red, so that the blood of the wounded would not show up. The white pantaloons worn by Napoleon and his troops, as well as by Wellington and his troops and Lord Nelson and his officers, were highly impractical. Yet for a long time there was no move to change them or any aspect of military uniforms. They looked dashing and that was what mattered. In the ball-room it was vital, as it still is, for officers to look splendid. In the dance halls and pubs it was no less important that the rank and file should out-do other men.

The heroic 'Thin Red Line' of British infantrymen, so dear to

Trumpeter in
Imperial French
cent-garde.
(Popular print)

legend, was a suicidal target in war. The lucky charms which all soldiers secrete about their persons, could not help them – the scarlet pea-jacket, very tight trousers, choking collar, the strange busby or, just as fantastic, the Boys' Brigade pill-box hat held on by a strap beneath the chin, were as archaic as they were impractical.

The British uniforms had not been designed to frighten French soldiers, yet this was achieved by accident. The kilts of the Scottish regiments, associated with their renowned pugnacity, terrified the French soldiers who described them as 'Ladies from Hell'. In the 1914–18 war the Scottish kilts had the same effect on German soldiers. Unfamiliarity can be an important weapon – we all tend to be afraid of what is new to us.

The Boer War later brought in the long reign of khaki and puttees (both Indian words). Though the new uniform was still too tight, it was possible to fight in it, and it offered some approach to camouflage compared to the old scarlet tunics. But a cloth helmet shaped like a topee was still being worn. There were many needless deaths in the 1914–18 First World War, and a tremendous outcry

121

Military glory.
(Lithograph by Daumier)

from members of Parliament in the House of Commons, before the War Office allowed the 'tin hat' to be issued, which saved thousands of deaths from shrapnel.

In the armed forces hair is as strictly controlled as in prison. T. E. Lawrence, who had enlisted under an assumed name as an ordinary ranker, describes what it looked like in the R.A.F. before 1939 in *The Mint*:

Recruits' heads were clipped to the blood and pale as scalp's pink. Even senior men were compelled to have pig's bristles like ours at the neck: but on top their hair was very long, and greased tightly to their skulls, so as to fit inconspicuously under their caps. *Airmen will risk any punishment rather than go cropped like soldiers.*

The Second World War (1939–45) – twenty years later – proved to be a war as much on civilians as between armies. Those women in England not in official uniform contrived a 'war dress' of their own which quickly became standardized: a kerchief, either tied under the chin or twisted into a turban, a sweater (hand-knitted in shelters), trousers, clumpy footwear – in summer a blouse without a sweater. For children the 'siren suit' (popularized by Winston Churchill) was a godsend – hooded against chill nights in shelters, long and warm, it was a shelter in itself. Better-off children wore them in better materials but it was still a siren suit, brilliantly devised for its purpose and still going strong as a winter garment.

Just as it is the winning army in a war which sets the fashions afterwards James Laver believes that the post 1914–18 war toque derived from the tin hat, and that the long reign of beige was because it resembled a version of khaki dye – the garment which achieved lasting popularity after the second world war was the duffle coat.

This was originally a naval 'arctic' garment, immortalized for its service on convoy ships in icy waters. After the war it was bought by young (and old) people from army surplus stores – for clothes rationing continued for a long time. The duffle proved so popular for its warmth, good lining, excellent pockets, practical hood, for its endearing toggle fastenings and modest price, that both sexes and all children have continued to wear it ever since – the rich in expensive materials with horn toggles, ordinary people in strong cloth with wooden toggles.

Sir Philip Sidney
(Gray's Inn Collection)

123

Evacuation scene, 1939.
(Lithograph by Pearl
Binder)

What can the British soldier wear today, to defend his country in case of highly technological nuclear war? What uniform can we devise, when a button pressed thousands of miles away can trigger off the nuclear destruction of whole cities and everybody in them? The approved uniform of the soldier of today is heavily camouflaged, with nets and painted patterns to deceive the eye. This uniform is hung about with various machines to receive and send out messages, – with grenades, mines, quick-firing guns, and belts of ammunition.

124

Peace dress Has not the time come for us to think less about war but about the blessings and the maintaining of peace?

The dress of soldiers and the war-minded is stiff. Its lines are angular. It has no curves. Its shoulders are squared. It is Yang-Macho.

The dress of peace-lovers, on the other hand, is soft, unemphatic, tranquil, rounded, not aggressively sexual. Nor is it costly. Whatever followers may do and wear in their name (and what some 'Christians' have done to Christianity) that is how it started.

Gautama Buddha, born into the princely ruling Sakya tribe of a small North Indian family was a devout Hindu. His search for truth led him to preach the reform of Hinduism, which had become harsh, over-concerned with ritual trivia, giving Hindu Brahmin priests almost divine power and status. Buddha was opposed to caste which, so far from being indigenous to India, had been forced upon her by conquerors determined to 'divide and rule'.

Eventually the powerful Brahmin Hindu priests contrived to drive Buddhism out of India in order to preserve their own authority and the caste system. One or two pockets of Buddhism remained, including a dwindling sect of nuns and monks living near the foothills of Nepal. But Buddhism took strong root in Tibet. It was devoutly studied in Tibetan monasteries, whence it was taken to China (to become a strong force there for thousands of years), to Japan, Burma, Thailand, and later to Ceylon (Sri Lanka). What is outstanding in Buddhism is the love of Peace and practice of kindness to all living things. It is an intellectual religion, yet it has immense popular appeal.

Early sculptures of Buddha show him serene, faintly smiling, robed, one shoulder bare, in soft folds. Buddha had been married to a beautiful wife and had fathered a fine son. These he gave up along with his princely life, when the compulsion came to him to seek out a way to help human beings in their anguished lives. People who are Buddhists interpret his findings in all sorts of ways, but the message of peace is basic. They care for orphans, rescue animals, live simply – try to be calm and always loving. Some statues of the reclining Buddha are as long as a street, others are mountain-high, some are of gold or jade. Many feature snail-curls* all over his head made of turquoise. There are now many different Buddhist sects, and some temples have rooms full of repeated Buddhas – to make stronger magic. But his robe is always simple.

King Solomon has remained a legend far beyond his time and

* According to the legend, the snails, grateful to the Lord Buddha for protecting all living creatures, covered his shorn head with their bodies to shield him from the hot sun.

125

place. His great achievement lay in building the magnificent Temple (which the Romans later destroyed). What he accomplished (though not for long) was peace between Israel and her quarrelsome neighbouring countries.

Time was not on his side. He moved too fast trying to bring tribal uncultured Israel into the great world of rich and powerful countries. He drove his people too hard – forced labour, heavy taxes etc, when all they had or wanted perhaps was their invisible God. He had to buy from the Phoenicians and when the day of reckoning came, they refused to take gold and silver payment, demanding land instead, and they took possession of vital frontier towns. The two ends of Israel refused to cooperate and Israel broke up. By then Solomon was dead but the legend of Solomon remained, that he had made peace between Israel and her warring neighbours – not just *preached* it. In a practical way he showed that peace was not an idle dream.

One extremely important edict he introduced (very unpopular with his suspicious and single-minded subjects) was that all ambassadors and representatives of foreign countries in Jerusalem should be free to worship their own Gods (idolatrous or not) – and have their own Temples to worship in. This attitude was much ahead of its time but of a piece with his practical ideas for avoiding war. How did he dress? An exception to the simple garb of the peace-lover, he dressed with the utmost luxury – to match his gorgeous Palaces with their gorgeous appointments.

Asoka was the mighty Indian Emperor (born 304 BC) who, visiting the battlefield after a great victory (after a two-year war) against Kalinga, by the Bay of Bengal, saw for himself the horrors of war, and determined to devote his life and influence to the cause of peace. He put himself in touch with the dwindling group of forgotten Buddhist monks and nuns near Nepal (who related to him Buddha's ideas in his own words). He married a wife from Buddha's own Sakya tribe, met and exchanged ideas with learned men from other countries – including classical Greece. Then he disbanded his armies and, reducing his life-style to extreme simplicity, preached and practised the blessings of Peace throughout his vast territories and at every frontier.

'Moral force' was his weapon. He had his ideas engraved on rocks and pillars throughout India. His propaganda was clear, practical and concerned. He advocated the planting of food and medicinal trees so that people might eat and be cured of sickness, human and animal hospitals (which still exist in India) and the practice of dharma (non-violence).

In his early years as emperor he wore robes and crown of the utmost gorgeousness. As his Buddhist convictions grew, however, his robes grew simpler, and simpler. In his last years his servants had to beg him not to confine himself to one well-worn shabby garment.

St Francis of Assisi renounced his inherited riches for love of Jesus and his lessons. Today his preoccupation with nature (Sister moon – Brother sun – the trees – the flowers – the animals – the insects) has an enormously strong appeal to ecologists and the young especially. He loved his fellow men and burned to open their eyes to the beauty of the world and the honour he felt at being allowed to enjoy it. *He used to wear the robe of the order he founded – a simple brown hooded robe with a rope girdle.* Franciscan monks still wear it today.

William Penn is important in English history and Quaker annals

William Penn, aged 22, as a soldier in Ireland. (Archives of the Society of Friends)

127

Dressing Up
Dressing Down

for his active service to peace and justice. He was born to a rich mercantile family who planned to make a courtier of him, for Charles II liked him, a sure avenue to advancement. He became a soldier and was sent to Ireland where, as an officer, he was involved in active fighting. The experience changed his life. He could see no purpose in killing. He found himself totally against war. He met George Fox, founder of the Quaker Sect (who had started life as a shepherd) – a practical visionary who appealed (as did Christ whom he served) to the poor.

Penn's family pleaded with William not to throw away his chances in life for certain persecution and prison. The King (sure that Penn would succumb to the pleasures of the Court of Louis XIV) sent him off there. Penn, however, while putting in a polite appearance at Versailles, found a protestant pastor to help his religious understanding. On his return to England his preaching and defence of the Quakers landed him in prison. He defended the Quakers in a court

William Penn in old age
(Archives of the Society
of Friends)

128

action and actually (by interceding for the jury being bullied by a reactionary judge) got the law changed. But at last he decided that it would be better for the persecuted Quakers to leave England and try their luck elsewhere. America was a possible refuge. Penn discussed this plan with the Quakers who agreed to let him try to persuade King Charles to let them go. They had no money to pay King Charles for 'a tract of land' in his American colony. However the King owed the Penn family £1,600. Penn petitioned for a tract of land and permission to take a colony of Quakers there to cultivate it – in return for the £1,600 which the King owed his family. The King, still obsessed with the ancient dream of Eldorado, agreed on condition that any gold discovered would belong to the Crown, and asked what name Penn proposed to call this new territory. Penn replied '*Sylvania, Sire*' whereupon the King, not displeased to get Penn out of his way, urged, 'No. Not Sylvania – Pennsylvania'.

When Penn arrived in America with his family, his Quaker friends and his great plans for founding an ideal colony, he found that there were Red Indians there already. Penn got to know them, learned their language, became friends with them; he was deeply impressed by their devotion to their pagan religion.

The Indians, a notably athletic people, for their part appreciated Penn's physical strength and agility. There is a legend that they ran a race against each other which Penn won. They agreed to 'sell' Penn land, to settle and cultivate, made their wampum (beadwork) agreement which both sides kept and (when everything went wrong after Penn had to return to England where the Quakers were again being persecuted) they never lost their faith in Penn. Even after they had been cheated and tricked of their lands and driven into exile in Canada they still kept their wampum agreement to remind them of this one white man they trusted. But they did not just remember him and honour him. Later, when the strained situation broke into war, the Indians marked all Quaker houses, so that they should not be touched when they set fire to the white men's houses and killed those inside.

And later still – after Penn had died – in difficulties, having been cheated of his estate and saddled with debt by a rascally steward – his widow retired to their farmhouse 'Jordans' (in Buckinghamshire, and still a Quaker Centre). One bitter winter's night there was a knocking on the door. Out of the whirling snow-storm came three tall Indian chiefs, wrapped in deerskins. They had heard from so far away that their true friend Penn had died and they had somehow made their way across America, over the Atlantic ocean into Buckinghamshire to see his widow. They had brought her a present – it was a mantle made of many small pieces of different furs, beautifully stitched together in their own tribal patterns. They told her his Red Indian friends had made it for her 'to protect her now that her good husband had gone'.

Penn had admirable ideas, well ahead of his time on education, town planning, government – all inspired by his deep spiritual faith. But what of Quaker Dress?

Voltaire, when he visited England (the land of freedom as he thought) found Quaker dress rather comic. What the Quakers thought of his fashionable long curly wig, embroidered satin dress, high heeled shoes and costly lace ruffles is not recorded. He was friendly. That sufficed.

Quaker dress, as George Fox conceived it, was a simple dress, shorn of fashionable clutter and extravagance. Quakers did not wear black because it was expensive, requiring many dyeings. Mourning dress was against their principles. Their funerals were very simple, as they still are. They wore grey, beige, yellow-and-grey. A plain coat, shallow hat, plain breeches, knitted hose, strong shoes. No sword. Fox himself (a poor man) made his own breeches out of leather (since he was often imprisoned, he found that they kept out the fleas and bugs best). Quaker linen was always spotless – a 'must'. Quaker women wore a plain bodice/jacket and gathered skirt – white linen cap apron and wide collar – outside a felt hat over the cap and plain cape. George Fox's wife, widow of a judge, preferred to wear a red cloak, but was so loved and popular that criticism soon died down.

A Quakerly word of warning from Margaret Fell in the seventeenth century: 'It is a dangerous thing to lead young friends much into the observation of outward things, which may easily be done, for they can soon get into an outward garb to be all alike outwardly, but this will not make them true Christians.' She was talking about Fashion.

Protest dress We are now living in a nightmare world where war can mean total extermination of life. Nuclear contamination is known to be biologically disastrous. Citizens in Britain and the USA (to start with) are urged in that event to go into hiding, like moles, in special shelters under ground.

The explosion of the first atomic bomb on Japan in 1945 (why was the second one necessary?) caused revulsion throughout the world.

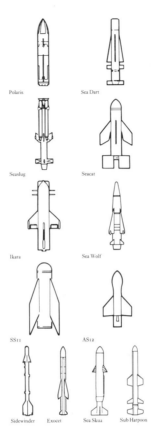

Polaris Sea Dart

Seaslug Seacat

Ikara Sea Wolf

SS11 AS12

Sidewinder Exocet Sea Skua Sub Harpoon

Poster from a recruitment office

The formation of CND, in 1958, was a grass-roots and world-wide reaction to the proliferation of even more powerful bombs.

The Campaign for Nuclear Disarmament (its badge the famous cross with dropped arms set within a circle, white on black or black on white; the logo is simply morse for CND) attracted people of all ages and *all classes* (something new for England). Their first march was to Aldermaston (then the English centre for nuclear research) from London: later marches reversed the direction so that the final rally at the end of the march could take place in traditional Trafalgar Square. The marchers carried banners denouncing the nuclear bomb and urging peace. They wore duffle coats, trousers, woollen jerseys. The girls wore pony-tails. Many young parents pushed prams the whole way. Everyone wore several badges. They also carried sandwiches and dry socks. The rain pelted down. The journalists sneered.

Contingents from other countries, including America, joined this and later marches. The police, ready for trouble, marched alongside

131

CND old lady on duty with Peace Army, Greenham Common

but there was no trouble – not yet. That came later with the 'sit-ins'. Women's 'sit-ins' (proliferating in America and all over Europe) have been going on in England since 1981, in groups from a few dozen to 10,000 and – on 12 December 1982 – 30,000 at Cruise missile bases.

More practical than their ancestors the Suffragettes (who handicapped themselves in the huge hats and hobble skirts of their day) they wear warm sweaters and scarves, waterproof anoraks, woollen ski caps and wellingtons. Their children wear 'siren-suits'. Conditions on the sites can be grim – especially in the icy rain and mud of winter.

The law does not want to make martyrs of these women. They are fined and they at once return to their 'sit-in'. Clearly they are not hooligans – not punks – not bored youths intent on a fight.

However, the situation is changing. *Dr Strangelove* is now old hat. DARPA, the Defence Avoidance Research Projects Agency of the U.S. Government, has already begun to develop the new super-computers which can, in the words of Dr Robert Cooper, 'act alone, can plan, strategise, employ resources and do the things that human beings normally do in a more leisurely paced engagement.'

132

(Above) The March of
Labour in East London.
(Scraperboard by
Dan Jones)

Miners' picket, 1974.
(Painting by Dan Jones)

* Two articles by Tom
Mangold in *The Listener*
(September 8th and
September 15th 1983).

This project is already well under way. 'It will have superspeed computation in the range of one billion to one trillion instructions per second' using the revolutionary molecular system. It would simply need one finger on the handle to set it all off – and this finger 'would have considerably less than *250 seconds* to decide and act.' And the latest missile is to attack enemy missiles in the stratosphere when it is perfected.*

We are outdoing *Star Wars* now. The women's 'sit-ins' have made their point, but the time has come, surely for them to pack up their tattered plastic covers, their children, and go home to begin the real protest. Since men are biologically directed to aggression, it is the women who are biologically directed to *preservation*, who must and should take over.

It was the common people of China who, feeling that Buddha had become too abstract and lofty, invented the goddess Kuan Yin, the beautiful caring Goddess of Mercy, who, hearing a child cry, turned back from entering Nirvana in order to comfort it.

The Flower of
Compassion, Buddhist
symbol (Tibet)

9 *Who Sets the Fashion?*

Do male couturiers *like* women?
I often get the impression that they don't.
Alison Settle

'Heaven' dance club.
(Drawing by Pearl
Binder)

In countries where the social order is static, dress remains static.
From emperor to slave everyone knows his or her place.

* These are not jokes.
They were serious 19th century English hymns.

God Bless the Squire and his relations
And keep us in our proper stations*

Though I am but poor and mean
I can teach the rich to love me
If I'm modest neat and clean
And submit when they reprove me*

136

Who Sets the Fashion?

What must be worn, from birth to death, is laid down in the greatest detail by strict Sumptuary Laws which none dare disobey. Any deviation threatens the stability of the Social Order. The king, therefore, wears his decreed regalia, the Queen her decreed regalia – robes which are as fixed and unalterable as are those of each grade of their subjects.

But the King's mistress, being outside society, is also outside the Sumptuary Laws. She can dress how she likes. And since it is in her own interest to make herself pleasing to her royal lover, she will invent seductive items of dress and seductive ways of wearing them. Gradually, then, these will penetrate the Sumptuary Laws, and the noble ladies of the Court will adopt them. Then the King's mistress will invent something new to wear.

This, according to James Laver, is how fashion began in the courts of medieval France. Later many new fashions were similarly launched by expensive high-class brothels (known by politer names) for they, too, were 'outside' society and existed by pleasing the men who paid the bills.*

Consider the unique opportunities brothels provide for understanding and catering for the fantasies of their clients. Once a man of substance was safely married and had children (especially the essential sons) he had done his family duty and was 'free' to seek his pleasures elsewhere. China had her system of concubinage, Japan her geishas, but Europe has generally preferred brothels.

* *Greensleeves* (now so popular with girls' schools' choirs) is a lament from the Middle Ages and certainly about a prostitute. Green, the colour of unfaithfulness then as now, was an unlucky colour in England. Was it associated with enemy saracens in the Crusades? Green is still the colour of the Prophet. In our time the bad luck may be associated with arsenic – used or believed to be used in colouring sweets, wallpaper and dress materials.

Venetian courtesan wearing breeches and stilt shoes, 16th century. (Racinet)

Hairdresser's signboard
(West Africa)

Brothels, almost scientifically, created the various styles of women (and youths) of whom men dreamed, and they dressed them in accordance with those dreams. The sexual obsessions of men are many and varied, but essentially it is the historic setting that changes, not the fantasies. What do men seek in this sexual dream-world? First, the mother-figure (earth mother, Eve, fertility goddess) plump, comforting, with large breasts: then, the cruel governess; the immature young virgin (specialists cater to paedophiliacs); the faithful sister; the perpetual bride; the experienced widow; the cripple; the knowing, or the innocent young schoolboy; the exotic Black Princess; the suffering masochistic women. Some men can only be turned on by a woman travelling alone in a railway carriage; others only by the wife of their best friend.

All these obsessions, like actresses in a play, need appropriate dress – not only the right clothes but hairdressing, manner of moving, of wearing the garments of obsession. This is the very root of fashion – the same dreams told and retold. For thousands of years of dress have produced myriad ways of making a woman (or a man) look fatter or thinner, taller or shorter, powerful or frail, mature or immature, what you will.

Fashions have been set by military victories. In 1477, when the Swiss routed the Duke of Burgundy at Nantes, the tattered victorious Swiss soldiers tore up the captured silk French banners to stuff their ragged shirts. It was this silk, protruding at every hole, which created 'slashings'.

Once launched, no amount of inconvenience matters, the new fashion is secure until driven out by the next wave. Staircases have been altered to permit passage of farthingales; and sedan-chairs have had apertures cut in their ceilings to allow tall feathered headdresses to be accommodated. When even this did not suffice, grand ladies preferred to travel kneeling down in their sedan-chair rather than change their hair-style. In 1794 *The Times* reported that feathers were '1½ yards high' and a new coach was being constructed so that the ladies sat in a well 'looking out between the spokes of the wheel'. At this time too, lady friends of Charles James Fox would display their hostility to his opponent William Pitt by wearing a fox tail in their hat or bonnet. Were they aware of its secret magic power?

Other military influences were: the Steenkirk neckcloth, named after the battle in 1692; the toque; the duffle coat; while the Duke of Wellington inspired the waterproof top-boots (which in the

French aristocratic
hairdressing prior to the
French Revolution.
(Racinet)

provinces in my youth used to be called 'Bluchers'). Today Che Guevara is still copied by would-be revolutionaries in many countries. Why? There is magic in success (and martyrdom).

Actresses, film stars, royalty, all may set fashions if their public image is strong enough – Sarah Bernhardt launched the Japanese paper parasol in Europe, and Gladys Cooper (the heroine of millions of picture-postcards) created the classic type of cool British beauty – described by Noel Coward as 'dressed in shell pink at garden parties', while Elvis Presley's followers still imitate his tight trousers, and Mick Jagger's fans his circus glitter.

Even protest dress can take many shapes. Fashionable dress-designers have been influenced by the contemporary 'sit-in' demonstrations. In costly creations they now offer dun-coloured heavy woollen garments, lopped trousers, leg warmers, heavy footwear, pulled-down felt hats – all perfect sit-in dress for the luxury market.

Today too every street market in England sells cheap copies of the Princess of Wales' flouncy blouses to young girls who save up, hoping that some of the royal magic will rub off on them.

Male dress today

But Elvis Presley and Mick Jagger and the newer pop idols, cannot be copied by the majority of young men working in offices and banks. Some admittedly will dye their hair and paint themselves into 'punks' after work each day; but like other office workers they have to wear to work dress that, surely, is unbecoming, unflattering, unmanly, uncomfortable and dear at any price.

The famous Savile Row styling is not what it was. The Englishman's hat is now nondescript – and usually non-existent. The city's bowler hat is usually only seen, if seen at all, worn defiantly in torrid weather. The stiff collar is uncomfortable – the soft collar sloppy.

140

The necktie has come down to us from the Roman occupation, when Roman soldiers, unused to the damp chilly English climate, constantly caught colds and developed pneumonia until they were issued a *focale* to wrap round their throats – and this eventually dwindled into the necktie. Narrow or wide, discreet or flamboyant, it does little for the wearer except perhaps advertise that he belongs to some club or group or wishes to appear that he does. In such guise the strong male neck has no chance; and if the neck is not strong it looks even worse in collar and tie.

The male jacket is aesthetically all wrong. What is more becoming, is when the horizontal line for both male and female dress by-passes the waist. The waist is best ignored. The coat should be cut much higher, giving the leg line more prominence (for young men) or much lower (giving older men dignity).

Waistcoats can be purposeful, dashing, useful, jaunty, worn buttoned or unbuttoned, but they look best without a jacket. Trousers, however, have become a bad joke – the hitching up before sitting has become a nervous tick – an obsessive act which seems to affect all men of all ages in England as to whether the flies are fastened properly, grows stronger with every domestic political or industrial crisis. Can this be the race who once revelled in codpieces? If tightly cut the trousers are uncomfortable, if loosely cut they look shapeless. Ordinary male shoes have little individuality. Male raincoats are simply drab. Can we wonder that youths settled for blue jeans and blue jeans only?

Englishmen are slow to change. John Betjeman once, with an indescribably daring/audacious/nervous look, quickly opened his jacket to reveal to me a bright red silk lining. A ray of hope? Could this hidden flash of red, the lucky magic colour of courage, be the beginning? In China the wicker field-hats of peasants and the black silk teapot-lid caps of old grandfathers are all lined with red. But, alas, no. It was not.

What we all want, surely, is that English youths and men should look manly, comfortable and make the most of themselves. They pay a lot for their clothes. It is time their clothes repaid them. All men, even short or thin men, look better in full evening dress – the high waist in front, the tails floating at the back, the waist by-passed. This is now very rarely worn, except for provincial mayors' inaugural Balls and for grand occasions at Buckingham Palace.

The distinguished French dress historian Professeur Boucher once told me that in his opinion the revolution we all long for in

141

European male dress will probably come about through sport – men now having for several reasons more leisure to play.* The young designers, perhaps as a result of this, are graduating from our excellent English Dress Design Schools with clumsy-sinister designs for male dress – something between climbing gear for a Himalayan Expedition and a gangster's get-up. It is meant to be manly, but it is no more than television-butch.

Interestingly, one hundred years ago the London costers, very aware of their male image, though without the money to implement their ideals, evolved a strikingly manly dress: no collar – instead a bright silk neckcloth or 'Kingsman'; the coat, longer than today, cut bell-shape – that is fitting at, or slightly above waist level, then widening to a full 'skirt'; trousers close fitting to the knee similarly belling out to the ankle; waistcoat – a great joy – closely buttoned with many little pockets on either side, all buttoned, either pearl or smoked pearl; cap close-fitting, or sometimes a jocular bowler (not always black), maybe dashingly sporting a wreath of roses. A Dickensian dress, and it brightened up the grey dull city and gladdened the hearts of every woman who bought ½lb. of sprouts or a potted geranium from their beautifully laid-out barrows.

After the second world war, the well-to-do young officers returning from ship or regiment and longing to be out of uniform, began to wear slightly narrow trousers and fancy waistcoats (called 'Edwardian', which was inaccurate). Savile Row, with its traditional devotion to Beau Brummell's expensive sobriety and perfect cut, produced beautiful waistcoats in black brocade or rich moirés with expensive unobtrusive buttons. Something was clearly starting.

But the East End lads, also longing for a change to something more exciting, seized on this new idea – and immediately the Charing Cross Road was filled with 'teddy boy' shops selling very bright fancy rayon 'brocaded' waistcoats, 'drain-pipe' trousers and light loose jackets. With these went very thick-soled clumpy shoes. These lads, saving up hard could still only afford to buy one item at a time, but it was enough. Savile Row, which must never be traduced and refused to be copied, withdrew from the contest.

But before long Savile Row came up with something else – anxious to please its rich young clients. This was *corduroy*, the ribbed cotton velvet of the labourer – originally worn by master chimney-sweeps – and traditionally worn tied below the knee. It was popular wear for dockers working in the docks.

Corduroy is a handsome, honest material, very hard-wearing,

142

Old clothes shop, 19th century. (George Cruikshank)

taking dye well. Savile Row began making fine *City* suits for their clients from *corduroy* – a daring and dashing innovation. Its young ex clients were delighted, wore them on City occasions, and the West End streets looked brighter. But the East Enders were outraged at this assault on their own special material. They too would not be copied. The battle raged silently for months. Then the East Enders withdrew, defeated. A great pity. Class bias is very powerful in England.

Since them the ethnic revolution has taken place, and English girls have learned to tress their long blonde hair in myriad Rastafarian plaits, while respectable matrons wear tea-gowns of violent African cotton prints whose designs they, perhaps fortunately, do not fully understand. And now the wheel has come full circle with what has happened to the 'Crysbach' – that 'little shirt' of the steel workers in the old Welsh steel rolling works. Made of flannel, it was collarless, and reached just below the belly. It had loose sleeves, with holes to let out the sweat.

The Sunday Times reported in April 1983:

> First it was the lumberjacket. Then it was wall-to-wall denim. And now the New York trendies have fallen for the ultimate in working-class chic . . . a traditional Welsh steelworker's vest. Mind you, this is no ordinary vest. Made in genuine Welsh flannel, it features attractive flared sleeves, a high neckline and, as a pièce de resistance, genuine holes under the arms to let the sweat drip out.
>
> It comes from the Melin Teifi woollen mill at Henllan, Dyfed, which is run by Raymond Jones and his wife Diane –
>
> The Jones family's vested interest started seven months ago when they took over the mill, which is housed in buildings put up as an Italian prisoner of war camp. From there the vests, which double as a women's leisure top or a men's outdoor smock, are air-freighted to Seattle to be marketed by a mail order company at about £26.
>
> The vests have not been worn by steelworkers since high technology and asbestos suits took over from more primitive methods, and Jones says that the 'ethnic touch' is an important selling point. This traditional aspect is reinforced in the mail order catalogue, which says the vests were designed to 'meet the rigorous needs of the steelworkers, facing the blazing heat of the furnace, with cold wind on his back'.

Revolutions have always demanded new styles of clothes for the new regime. France, after 1789, not only changed the calendar and installed a 'Goddess of Reason' to replace the Virgin Mary, but also

144

decided to introduce a completely new style of clothes for all French citizens. David, the famous artist, and Le Sueur, another artist, were ordered to design them. They tried very hard, inspired by antique Greek and Roman dress (and possibly Neapolitan opera). They drew designs for a range of garments, 'Suitable for youths, maidens, matrons, young men, older men, senators, aged men.'

The only difficulty was that they were all unwearable. True, French ladies, always adaptable, always with an eye on what might be done with unpromising material, quickly transformed the female

Design for a
Revolutionary male
dress, Paris, late 18th
century

145

Ionic/Doric *Chiton* into delightful flimsy chemises, open at the top, tied beneath the breasts, with 'three obligatory folds' (for good luck?) – which they wore with their hair curled. But the French men however, dismayed and embarrassed by David's and Le Sueur's 'designs for men' all refused to wear them, though one senatorial Himation survives at the Carnavalet Museum in Paris. Was it ever actually worn, one wonders? Senators, horrified at the thought of their skinny legs and unprepossessing knees being revealed to the merciless Paris jokes said 'no'. The workers and farmers, who felt they had done enough for the Revolution already, also refused. And the male dress which did take after the Revolution was based on English gentleman's dress – owing nothing at all to Greece and Rome but a great deal to Beau Brummell.

In 1934, in Moscow, a Soviet lady commissar asked me to advise her who was the best dress designer in England. She explained that the Soviet economy was improving and, as better consumer goods were being considered, they would like to do things properly. I told her Schiaparelli. Schiaparelli was presently invited to the Soviet Union and asked to design a dress 'suitable for a working woman'. Predictably, even for so unpredictable a designer, Schiaparelli designed a *'little black dress'*, one of those elegant nothings which need a skinny mannequin and a background of orchids to do it justice. Russian women, bread eaters, of course, especially the peasants, tend to be big, stout and matronly. The organizers were astounded and disappointed, but they paid Schiaparelli promptly and saw her off to the airport with every honour due to a distinguished visitor. What they had expected, heaven knows. Certainly not 'the little black nothing'. The dress was carefully put away and the idea abandoned.

However, a generation later Schiaparelli's 'little black nothing' (by now out of fashion everywhere) was taken up – and used to dress the wives of Soviet diplomats in the Western Capitals. Only of course made in the ampler sizes necessary for the Russian female figure – and never, never in black – but in royal blue satin. No longer a 'little Black Nothing' but a large shiny blue something else.

Each country creates its own style of dress, according to climate and occasion. Traditionally the Russian peasants wear a full-sleeved blouse under a low-cut sleeveless, full-skirted tunic. It suits them. It is as perfect for working in the fields as for nursing their babies. In 1960 a peasant family made the long journey from their village to a new department store in a northern Chinese city to buy a padded quilt – a

146

momentous decision involving the outlay of savings on the products of this strange new era of the machine. Grandfather, ready to give it a go, and wearing his black silk teapot-lid hat, led his family of sons, daughters and in-laws. The beaming salesgirl ran to fetch a quilt. Grandfather examined it professionally, tugged it hard – warp and weft – counted the cotton threads, wet his forefinger to test and taste the dye, smelt it, and finally stared hard at the printed design.

'Show me another, if you please.'

The salesgirl ran to fetch another quilt, then another and another. Grandfather subjected them all to the same meticulous treatment. Finally he gave judgment.

'Is this the best your new wonder machine can do?' he asked. 'In our village we make much better quilts ourselves – better cotton, stronger weaving, much faster dye, and we make and print much luckier patterns. And for this miserably machine-made quilt your store expects us to pay money? Mind you tell the director what I have said. Good morning, young miss!'

Was Grandfather, I wondered, trying to gain face by causing the director to lose face? No, it was more serious than that. It was the face of New China (which would be jeopardised by inferior workmanship), Grandfather was intent on saving. The machine must do *better*. At this same store I bought a pair of peasant trousers (the same as this family was wearing) – made of strong indigo cotton, adjustable tab, pockets where you need pockets, strong buttons firmly sewn on. More than twenty years later I am still wearing them.

Dress designers multiply today. They are important interpreters of the public's dream. But, as they will readily admit, they do not, cannot, force their own concepts on the public (though some do try). 'The Spirit of the Age', they believe, inspires them, and the best designers indeed are like fortune-tellers peering into a crystal ball. But fashion today has become an insane caucus race: two changes a year – backed by an army of photographers, reporters, graphic artists, dressers, models, make-up and perfume pushers, radio, television and press – seems to be heading in a distinctly voyou direction (though the wind may suddenly veer and a slight wind blow nostalgically backwards towards good tweeds, three rows of pearls and a pastel sweater in Scottish wool). 'Evening gowns' now hardly exist – a short violent dress with no back and a transparent front, suitable for a disco night out, seems to have taken its place. Punk-influenced dress creeps into all the collections, at fabulous prices.

147

'New Women' –
President of the Brighton
Golf Club, 1890s

*Who sets the
fashion?* Dress designers of talent and originality are more likely to be found (in all countries) amongst the unprivileged, of whom there are far greater numbers and whose perception and zest have not been blunted by a formal education or being crammed with other people's ideas. England is fortunate in this respect because the 1945 election opened up, besides the universities and schools of science, the great schools of design to talented youngsters from poor families and gave them grants for the sort of study their parents could not

148

afford. The results have been very exciting. Three outstanding such designers are: *Bill Gibb*, son of a Scottish crofter; *Zandra Rhodes*, daughter of a lorry driver; and *Bill Pashley*, son of a small pig farmer. Others, unfortunately, have been enticed away to Italy or Paris or the U.S.A.

These designers all make beautiful, original and wearable clothes, and make them themselves for particular clients. Zandra Rhodes also designs and prints her own fabrics. *Who sets the fashion now?* Laura Ashley's 'anti-fashion' simple Edwardian-style cotton dresses of neat Edwardian prints were an instant success. They were strong, well-made, and lasting. She now has branches all over the world but sells, arguably, too many other items besides clothes.

One remarkable and outstanding woman journalist who did make fashion partly because it was her life-work, but also because her interests were so wide (she became a brilliant war reporter in World War II) was the late Mrs Alison Settle. She edited *Vogue* for some years and also worked on *The Observer*. During the second world war she gave marvellous talks to working-class girls in munition factories all over the country. She studied the needs of the dress trade and persuaded English manufacturers to weave their woollen material in wider widths to the great benefit of themselves and the dress trade.

She 'discovered' Christian Dior before anyone else, and on *Vogue* gave the photographer/artist Cecil Beaton his first chance. At the same time she kept the artists going and in those days fashion artists were artists.

In 1934 Alison Settle sent me to Moscow to cover the Soviet Theatre Festival for *Vogue*; and to 'make a lot of drawings of Russian women on stage and off stage'. Which I did: engine drivers, street cleaners, cooks, stage directors, all huge, sturdy and plump. When, on my return, I unrolled my drawings in her office she examined them carefully, and said, '*Not* exactly the female figures we associate with *Vogue*, dear – still it makes a change'.

Later on I decided to go to the Crimea for a winter holiday – packing an old copy of *Vogue* in my suitcase. On the beach I made friends with some young Russian women, plump and pleasant in their holiday sarafans (cotton summer sleeveless frocks). They pored over my copy of *Vogue* – their first glimpse of the Capitalist World – especially the fashion drawings. 'Poor women,' they cried, 'they must be starving! You don't get enough bread in England!'

149

Vogue for very tall women, late 19th century. (du Maurier in *Punch*)

But another, slightly older and less plump woman, shook her head and sighed a Byronic sigh. 'NO! NO! Don't listen to them! They don't understand elegance. Of *course* it is chic to be thin. Myself, I suck lemons *every* night to make myself pale and interesting, with black shadows under my *eyes*!'

POSTSCRIPT

We Are What We Wear

Banaban girl dancer.
(Lithograph by Pearl
Binder)

152

Postscript During the winter of 1973, which I spent on the Fiji Island of Rambi, I met a man who was old and in the last stages of tuberculosis. I did not recognise him in his clean blue shirt and well pressed shabby white trousers, and he was very poor, and too proud to allow me to visit him in his small hut. In fact I *had* seen him before, dancing wrapped in the green palm-leaves and rattling sea-shells of a Banaban Sea God, with disordered white hair and strange inhuman gestures. His name was Tawaka Kekenima Tang. He was choreographer and leading male dancer of the newly-revived Banaban dancers.

The Banaban's real home was the equatorial island of Banaba or Ocean Island. They were driven from there by the exploitation of phosphate by the BPC (British Phosphate Company), which destroyed their food trees (like the coconut and pandanus) and their four villages, Uma, Tabiang, Tapwewa and the sacred village of Buakonikai.

Ocean Island, 3 miles by 2 miles, lies on the equator. The climate is hot and unchanging. The Pacific Ocean, here at its deepest, abounds in fish, some extremely large. Yet lack of water is a serious problem on Ocean Island.

The Banabans were pagan, educating their youths on their coral terraces by the seashore in sun-magic (kouti), training them to catch the sacred frigate birds (symbols of the sun) by lassooing them on the wing and taming them, and also teaching the youths their Banaban history, training them for fishing and for marriage.

The women, kept apart, prepared food, smoked palm leaf for their kilts, and learned and practised the méké (gesture) dances by which their priest related their legends and history. Two strict Banaban pagan life-preserving laws were:-

1 *No Killing* Bloodshed would stain their island and offend their revered goddess Tetuabine.

2 *No Sails* were permitted on their canoes. The violent winds and immense distances of the Pacific making return impossible if a Banaban fisherman daringly sailed too far out.

In 1886 Captain Walkup, an American methodist missionary, arrived on Ocean Island. He had previously failed as a boxer and as a sea captain. Now he was determined to make a good living from

153

the Banabans. He taught them that they were sinful and must repent by fines and prayers.

E. Carlyon Eliot, then Resident Commissioner on Ocean Island, wrote: 'The missionaries worked hand in glove with the traders by telling the natives they should "cover their nakedness" . . . I found for example an absurd missionary law . . . A child, as soon as it could stand, must be clad in a loincloth. In return all the missionaries received their goods at cost price.'

Before long the Banabans had lost their own Banaban language, were singing hymns in Gilbertese, *they had stopped dancing* because Walkup forbade it, and were covering themselves because he said it was sinful not to. They were producing copra for him. Also there was a bigger mission on the bigger island of the Gilberts – so the Banaban language was swept away and the Gilbertese language introduced to make administration easier.

Then in 1900, Albert Ellis, a New Zealander working from Australia, came to complete their undoing by his discovery and exploitation of their phosphate. However not all the Banabans had become Christians. A few preferred to remain faithful to their old pagan religion.

Ocean Island was now taken over by the British, first as a dependency, then as a colony. Arthur Grimble, who arrived just before 1914, wrote:

> What stood out initially was a dreadful corrugated-iron factory building above the waterfront, from which enormous clouds of dust were being thrown sky-high. It was the crushing mill of the Company, busy pulverising its daily quota of a thousand tons of phosphate rock for the export market. The dust it flung out drifted heavily down the still air to load all the greenery on the Island's flank with a grey pall.

On Rambi, their island of exile, bought with their own money, the Banabans, like the Jews yearning for their lost Jerusalem, mourned their ruined homeland, living the life of exiles, unable to settle.

Tawaka Kekenima Tang had brought a penny-ruled schoolboy exercise book with him. I did not realize its significance until later. It was his book of poems (which are magic songs, which in turn are dances), with the mékés (body language movements) meticulously indicated by neat little signs. Immediately we were on such an exact wave-length that we hardly needed Pastor Tebuke's service as translator – all the more because Tebuke (a third generation Methodist pastor) was himself astonished at what Tawaka Kekenima Tang had to tell me.

The four Banaban villages traditionally had produced a certain number of talented 'poets' who believed they had the gift of singing-dancing-poetry-magic. Of these the best had been chosen by the pagan High Priests for special training. It was rigorous, for these poets were to be the recorders of Banaban history and magic beliefs. This I knew had been so in the old days before Missionary Walkup arrived. What Takawa Kekenima Tang now had to tell us was that all this had continued in secret after the missionary's arrival – the teaching, the rituals, the lessons, the precious language, conveyable only by speech and movement, having no written form. In fact it continued right until the Banabans were driven from Ocean Island. From 1900 it went on steadily on the opposite side of the Island from the noisy dust-belching phosphate crushing-mill.

The initiation of the young poet, on a magically-chosen propitious night, was first presented to the pagan gods of Banaba just before dawn, crowned with a wreath of special leaves 'smoked' in a sacred fire. Now he was allowed to begin composing. Everything he composed was submitted to the High Priest for criticism and encouragement, for only the very best was going to be good enough.

The water-oriented moon played a vital part in these rituals. His first ritual of initiation took place at quarter moon – his second at half-moon, his third at three-quarter moon. His final full ritual of acceptance was conducted by full moon in the unseen presence of the entire Pantheon of Banaban Pagan Gods and Goddesses. By now the young poet was ready to take on the important task he had trained so long to undertake. He was to be the revered poet of Banaba, whose inspired words and music would be sung, danced and *remembered* over the generations, as indeed they are today.

All this tied in perfectly with the lunar movements of Pacific sea creatures whose fertility travels trace the Pacific ocean – where on hot remote seasonless islands it is the phases of the moon and not the temperature of the sea which triggers off mating urges. It also ties in with the earliest Tapa designs I had been copying in the museum in Suva. Now I could see they were clearly lunar.

'And what', I asked Tawaka Kekenima Tang 'was the High Priest looking for in these essays in creative composition? Was it syntax, rhyme, content?'

'No' he replied, shooting a piercing glance at me, 'not at all. Anyone can learn such things. The High Priest was not giving a lesson to a schoolboy. He was assisting the birth of our most

155

important Banabans – our Bards who received and transmitted our history to the future. Every word, every movement, every note, like the palm leaves, the bark fibre, the fresh flowers, the frigate-bird feathers, and the pure white seashells of our pagan dance dress, had to be of the highest and purest quality . . .'

'What,' he insisted, 'the High Priest was looking for and looking for, and looking for was this:

'*TRUTH TO REALITY – ALL AND ONLY* that which is useful to LIFE.' In order to safeguard life – to enable life to continue, nothing *irrelevant* was ever allowed to intrude. That, he said was the Banaban pagan religion. What the young Bard had to learn to express was,
'*NEVER TO TRIVIALISE LIFE*'

Finally, at full moon, he was presented to the entire Pantheon of Banaban Gods totally naked so that nothing should come between him and the flow of their magic power. The communication had to be absolute.

Then I realised who he was. Takawa Kekenima Tang, this proud exhausted old man, was the last Banaban pagan High Priest. He died soon afterwards. But he had passed on to me his pagan warning:

The poet, subjecting himself naked to the magic power of the full moon on that remote little island, is Man in the Universe. We start our lives naked. What we dress ourselves in must never be rubbished, for our clothes express us and we are part of nature.

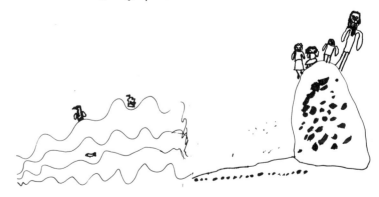

we saw a cormorant in the sea and it had oil on its feathers the cormornt is trying to fly

Cormorants crippled
with oil on their wings.
(Drawn by Polly Jones)

INDEX

Aborigines: symbols 2; *The Passing of the Aborigines* 9; body painting 12, 69; initiation ceremonies 15; executioner's slippers 51

Africa: lobolo 38; jewellery 56–7; Sumptuary Laws 69; witchdoctor 95; rainmaker 95

animals: mimicry in dress 26–8

Arabian Nights, The 8, 17, 40

Arabs: attitude to women 42–3; jewellery 56–7; art 107

armour 118–19

Ashley, Laura 149

Asoka, Emperor 126–7

babies: girls 32–3; charms 33–5; boys disguised as girls 35

Banabans 153–6; hibiscus flower 35–6; funerals 47–8; poets 155

Bates, Daisy 112; *The Passing of the Aborigines* 9, 14–15

Batik 108

Bernhardt, Sarah 140

body decoration 11–20; aborigines 12–15; painting 12–17; tattooing 17–20; kelloid 20; regulation of 69–70

Borneo 21

boys: disguised as girls 35

brothels 137–9

Buddhism: symbolism of Buddha 54–5; religious dress 98–9; peace dress 125

bum-roll 72

Campaign for Nuclear Disarmament 131

Carrib Indians 21

Catlin, George 28, 95

charms: childbirth 33

cheongsam 24

Chi'i-Lin 6

childbirth 30–5; taboos 31; rituals 31–2; charms 33; bastards 37–8

China: dragon 6, 92; Chi'i-Lin 6; traditional opera 15; foot-binding 21–2; moon-face 22; childbirth 32–3; chastity 39; weddings 39; wedding bed 41; death ceremonies 45–7; mourning dress 48; jewellery 55–6; status and dress 67–8; imperial robes 67–8, 98–100; national symbols 92

circumcision: male 21; female 21

class, *see* status

clowns 16

codpiece 70

colour symbolism 15–17

Confucius: on funeral ceremonial 46; on jade 56; rules of dress 100

Cooper, Gladys 140

corduroy 142–4

corset: female 23; male 26

costers 142; pearly kings 62–6

cowrie shells 56–7

Croft, Henry 62–3

Crowley, Robert: *One and Thirty Epigrammes* 72

crysbach 144

Dalai Lama 98

Davidson, Bill 66

death: funeral ceremonial 45–7; mourning 48–50

Defoe, Daniel 48–50

deformation, physical 21–6

Dickens, Charles: *David Copperfield* 24

Disraeli, Benjamin: *Sybil* 89

dress designers 147–8

Drew, Jane 28–9

duffle coat 123

England: mourning 48–50; medieval 70–1; Elizabethan 71–3; James I 73; Charles II 73–4; Royalists 74, 119; Quakers 74; Victorian 77; class 77–9; John Bull 90; Puritans 111;

157

Index

military dress 120–2; female war dress 123
Eskimos: children 34–5; ideal bride 39; funerals 47; evolution 82–3; shaman 96–7
ethnic fashion 144

fashion: origins of 137
feathers 26–8
Fiji: religious dress 105
folk-dress 87–90
folk-song 88–9
foot-binding 21–2
footwear: boots 23–4; heighteners 26; stilt shoes 26
Fox, George 74, 128
France: national symbol 90–2; wartime fashion 92; Napoleonic military dress 120; post-Revolutionary dress 144–6
Francis of Assisi, Saint 127
Frazer, Sir James: *The Golden Bough* 5
Freuchen, Peter: *Book of the Eskimos* 34, 82, 96–7

Gibb, Bill 149
Greek Orthodoxy: vestments 109
Gwynne, Nell 74
gypsies 113–14; funeral ceremonial 47; national identity 93; dress 114

Hair: dyeing 17; as virility symbol 120; military style 122–3
Haiti: Vevers 102–3; Voodoo 103
Hanway, James 57–8
Hawaii: 'Mother Hubbards' 105
Hindus: colour symbolism 16–17; childbirth 32; girls 32; funerals 47; religious dress 98; Kolem 100–2

India: arranged marriage 39; dowry 43; jewellery 53–4; caste 67
Indonesia: Batik patterns 108
Inglis, Hon. James: *Our New Zealand Cousins* 84–5
International Folklore Festival 89
Islams, *see* Muslims
Islamic art 107–8
Italy: chastity 39

Japan: western dress 93; military dress 120

jewellery 52–66; jade 55–6; unlucky 56; lucky 56–7; cowrie shells 56–7; teeth 61
Jews 114–15; circumcision 21; wedding 39; mourning 48; national identity 93; religious vestments 105–7; temple 107; 'sheitle' 115; prayer shawl 115; Yeshiva 115; Yemenites 115
John Bull 90

Kelloid marking 20
Kirkup, James: *Tropic Temper* 48

Laver, James 137
Lawrence, T. E.: *The Mint* 122–3
luck 7–9; jewellery 56–7

male dress, modern 140–4
Manners and Tone of Good Society 50, 74–7
Maoris: European influences 85–6
marriage 35–45; polygamy 31; dowry 38, 43; chastity 38–9; arranged 39; beds 41; of widows 50; and social class 78–9
Mexico: village dress 88
Middle Ages: Sumptuary Laws 70; armour 118–19; beginnings of fashion 137
military dress 118–24; corsets 26; influence on fashion 139–40
missionaries 84, 104–5, 111–13, 153–4
Muslims: colour symbolism 17; wedding dress 40; jewellery 57; Burqua 109

national dress: Scotland 87; Poland 87
national symbols 90–3
necktie 141

Padaung: neck-elongation 22
Païva 61
Panare Indians: missionising 87
Papua New Guinea: childbirth 31
Pashley, Bill 149
peace dress 125–30
Pearl, Cora 17
pearly king 62–6
Penn, William 127–30

158

Index

Persia: jewellery 57–8
phoenix 7
Plains Indian: animal totems 26–8; white man's influence 85–6; witch doctor 95; war dress 119–20
Poland: jewellery 57; national dress 87; Roman Catholicism 110
Polynesians: tattooing 69; European influences 84; dancing 104–5
Pritchett, V. S.: *A Taxi at the Door* 38
protest dress 130–5; and fashion 140
Puritanism 111

Quakers 74: William Penn 127–30; dress 130

Red Indians, *see* Plains Indians
religious ceremonial: dress 94–117; noise 98
Rhodes, Zandra 17, 149
Roman Catholicism: papal vestments 109–10
ruff 72–3

Samoa: coconut fibre mat 69
Schiaparelli 146
Scotland: bastards 37–8; national dress 87; Highland regiments 121
Settle, Alison 149
shaman 95–7
Sharp, Cecil 88–9

siren suit 123
slashings 139
Solomon, King 125–6
Soviet Union: national symbol 92; peasant dress 146
Spain: chastity 38–9
status 67–80; religious 111–12
Sumptuary Laws 68–70, 137; on remarriage of widow 50
surgery, cosmetic 24–6
symbols 4–7; colour 15–17; national 90–2

tattooing 17–20; 69
teddy boys 142
Tibet: jewellery 54–5; religious dress 98; Buddhism 125
toque 123

Uncle Sam 90
United States of America: national symbol 90

wedding: China 39; dress 39–40; royal 41–2
widowhood: remarriage 50
witch doctor 95
women, attitudes towards 42–5
Wu, Ching Tzu: *The Scholars* 33, 39

Yin-Yang 3, 92

159